Web Test Automation in Action: Volume 1

Hands-On Exercises with Selenium WebDriver and Playwright

Zhimin Zhan • Courtney Zhan

Web Test Automation in Action: Volume 1

Hands-On Exercises with Selenium WebDriver and Playwright

Zhimin Zhan, Courtney Zhan

ISBN 978-0-6480646-5-7

Contents

CONTENTS

CONTENTS

CONTENTS

Preface

Zhimin typically delivers web test automation training in the form of one-day group workshops or personalized one-on-one coaching. The primary audience for these sessions consists of manual software testers and developers—professionals who already possess foundational knowledge of software development, testing, HTML, or even basic programming skills.

Training IT Laymen: A New Challenge

In 2023, Zhimin began an experiment to train two complete novices in E2E Test Automation—individuals with no prior experience in software development. Their understanding of web technology was limited to basic web browsing, and they had neither the intention nor the desire to pursue careers in IT. Engaging such an audience posed a significant challenge: the traditional 8-hour training format was unsuitable, as it could overwhelm them or cause them to lose interest.

To address this, Zhimin designed a series of bite-sized training sessions. These short daily lessons, lasting 15–30 minutes each, included:

- A brief introduction to the topic.
- A simple, easy-to-understand test case with clearly outlined steps.
- Hands-on practice, with personalized coaching during the session.

The results were promising, demonstrating that even individuals with no prior IT background could grasp the basics of test automation through concise, focused learning.

Turning into a written format

In late 2023, a friend's nephew, a freshman majoring in computer science at a university in Sydney, expressed an interest in learning test automation. Zhimin suggested he begin with the following books:

- Practical Web Test Automation with Selenium WebDriver[1]

---

[1] https://leanpub.com/practical-web-test-automation

- Selenium WebDriver Recipes in Ruby[2]

Zhimin also shared details about the recent bite-sized training sessions designed for beginners, which he seemed had more interested in that approach. This motivated Zhimin to adapt the training exercises into a written, self-guided format.

Zhimin and Courtney published dozens of articles on Substack[3], which the IT freshman found helpful, commenting that the format was "quite easy to follow." Encouraged by this positive feedback, the material is now being expanded and developed into this book.

Why this book?

> "Test Automation is super practical. The best way to learn and master Test Automation is by doing many exercises, preferably guided high-quality exercises, hands-on." — Zhimin Zhan

One common reason many people struggle to master web test automation is the lack of high-quality, practical exercises. Testers new to automation often find themselves unable to handle real-world test scenarios when the test scripts become more complex than basic "hello-world" examples. This challenge leads to frustration, causing them to abandon test automation altogether and return to manual testing.

By completing a carefully designed set of exercises, testers can gain the skills needed to tackle more complex test scenarios and build the confidence to further incorporate test automation into their work.

This is the first of three volumes, each focusing on a different aspect:

- Volume 1 (*this book*): The Foundation.
- Volume 2: Enhancements for Designing Tests for Maintainability and High Efficiency, with Test Refactoring.
- Volume 3: Comprehensive, Real-World Test Scenarios.

---

[2]https://leanpub.com/selenium-recipes-in-ruby
[3]https://agileway.substack.com/s/selenium-webdriver-training-workshop

What's unique about this book?

1. **Bite-sized Learning: Small, Short, and Focused**

   Each session is designed with a specific focus and typically takes 15–20 minutes to complete. Test automation concepts and best practices are introduced gradually, with key knowledge points reinforced through repetition in subsequent sessions.

2. **Cover the top two leading web automation frameworks: Selenium Web-Driver and Playwright**

   Test automation is a cornerstone of Agile development. In 2003, Watir (Web Application Testing in Ruby) pioneered browser-based, end-to-end (functional) testing. Since then, numerous web automation frameworks have emerged and faded. Two decades later, Selenium WebDriver and Playwright remain the dominant frameworks[4] in the field.

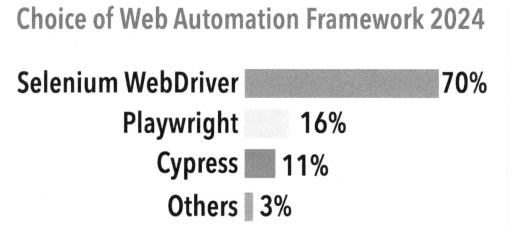

Figure 1. Two independent surveys conducted in late 2023 yielded similar results

The solutions for all the exercises in this book are in both Selenim WebDriver and Playwright, so readers can choose to learn either one or both.

---

[4]https://agileway.substack.com/p/selenium-webdriver-is-still-the-best

Readers familiar with my previous books and blog articles know that I am a strong advocate for using Selenium WebDriver with RSpec (Ruby) for web test automation. In this book, however, I also cover Playwright (TypeScript). This is where my daughter, Courtney Zhan, comes in. While she still prefers Selenium + RSpec, Courtney achieved an unprecedented level of test automation at a large telecom company during her 3-month internship, using Playwright.

Who should read this book?

Software professionals, from testers, programmers, software architects and agile coaches, who want to learn hands-on web test automation.

Prior experience with automated testing and programming is not necessary. Basic scripting knowledge will help, but again, not necessary.

How to read this book?

We strongly recommend readers to do the exercises through chapters in order. The solutions are provided on the book site, which also include screencasts. If you got stuck, refer to those resources.

Send us feedback

We would like to hear from you. Comments, suggestions, errors in the book and test/build scripts are all welcome. You can submit your feedback via the book website.

Zhimin Zhan and *Courtney Zhan*

Brisbane, Australia

1: Hello Web Test Automation

Web Test Automation is using automated scripts to drive a web app in a browser, i.e., Chrome, for testing.

Learning Objectives

1. View automated test execution in a Chrome browser
2. Install a test automation tool from scratch
3. Run an automated test

Tasks

Complete the tasks in sequential order. Each task in this book is designed to be straightforward and quick — typically taking a few minutes.

Task 1. View automation in action

During training sessions or the first coaching meeting, Zhimin typically begins with a live demonstration of test execution. Quite often, new automation learners were quite impressed, then Zhimin told them: "*You will be able to get all set up and run one test like me in under 10 minutes*". This would get the attendees excited. And minutes later, they would achieve just that!

Here is a video demonstrating the execution of an automated test in a Chrome browser.

Video 1: Execution of an Automated Web Test, YouTube[1]

Watch it to get a sense of how web test automation works in practice:

---

[1]https://youtu.be/kkPo1Xq17iM

1. Trigger a run in a test tool (or command line).
2. A Chrome browser is launched.
3. Drive the application (in the Chrome browser) quickly, 'using' the keyboard and mouse.
4. The Chrome browser is closed.

During on-premise training, Zhimin would try to demonstrate a test scenario relevant to the audience, showcasing how their daily tasks can be performed much more efficiently.

Task 2. Set up Test Automation Tool (for execution)

Setting up test automation from scratch can be simple and easy (in just a few minutes), if using the right tools.

Selenium WebDriver Ruby

We'll be writing Selenium WebDriver tests using the Ruby language in the TestWise IDE. If you have questions, be sure to check out the FAQ section at the end. For now, we encourage all participants to follow along with the steps, as our goal is to help you run your first automation in 10 minutes or less!

For Windows users, download the TestWise Ruby Edition[2]. If you're using macOS or Linux, install Ruby and Selenium libraries first, then proceed with the TestWise Standard Edition. Detailed set-up instructions can be found in the Appendix.

TestWise Ruby Edition = TestWise Standard Edition + Ruby + Testing Libraries

---

Launch TestWise without a license, and a popup window will appear for 10 seconds. Click the **Continue** button to proceed. You can still use TestWise and all it's features for free. You don't need to purchase a TestWise license to learn from this book or for

---
[2]https://agileway.com.au/testwise/downloads

casual use at work. TestWise can be used in free mode without a time limit, with the only restriction being the number of test executions allowed per launch.

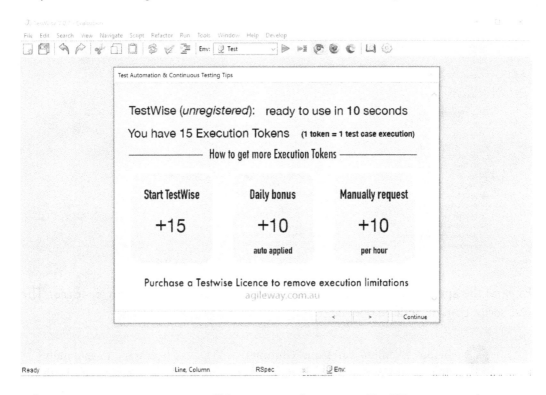

After 15 test executions, you will be prompted to restart TestWise — a quick process that takes just a few seconds.

TestWise comes a few sample projects. On the start screen, click "Open Sample Project (web app)".

You will see some folders (on the left), which contain the same set of tests for different languages.

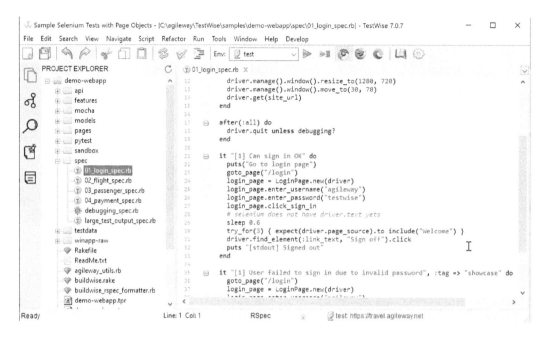

Expand the **spec** folder and click to open the test script file `01_login_spec.rb`. The test script content will be opened.

Before Selenium v4.11 and Chrome v115, it was necessary to manually download the matching ChromeDriver and add it to your PATH. With Selenium Manager, this process is now automated. However, it's useful to know the following just in case:

- To check your browser's version, go to `Help > About Google Chrome`.
- To verify the ChromeDriver version, run `chromedriver --version` in the command line.

Playwright TypeScript

Playwright, a relatively new web automation tool developed by Microsoft, has gained popularity in recent years. It supports multiple programming languages, including JavaScript, TypeScript, Python, Java, and .NET. In this book, we'll focus on the most commonly used Playwright binding: TypeScript.

> TypeScript is a superset of JavaScript that introduces static typing and other advanced features.

To get started quickly and easily with Playwright, I recommend using Visual Studio Code along with its the Playwright extension (from Microsoft, too). For instructions on using VS Code with Playwright, refer to the Appendix. That said, it's a good practice to understand how to install and run Playwright manually.

Installing Playwright with TypeScript yourself may take a bit longer, but it is still relatively straightforward.

1. **Install Node.js**

   Follow the instructions on the Node.js site. For macOS, `brew install node` using HomeBrew.

2. **Install Playwright Test package**

   ```
   npm install --global @playwright/test
   ```

3. **Install the browsers for Playwright**

   Unlike Selenium WebDriver, Playwright works exclusively with browser instances specifically built for Playwright. This means Playwright test execution does not completely replicate the end user's environment, but close enough.

   ```
   npx playwright install
   ```

   This will take a few minutes. You will see an output like below:

```
Downloading Chromium 125.0.6422.26 (playwright build v1117)
downloaded to /Users/ME/Library/Caches/ms-playwright/chromium-1117
Downloading Firefox 125.0.1 (playwright build v1449)
downloaded to /Users/ME/Library/Caches/ms-playwright/firefox-1449
Downloading Webkit 17.4 (playwright build v2003)
downloaded to /Users/ME/Library/Caches/ms-playwright/webkit-2003
```

Download the book sources at the book site. Unzip and you will find various folders under sources/playwright as example projects.

Task 3. Run one automated test yourself

Yes, you will run an automated test, which can be quite exciting for those doing it for the first time.

For complete beginners, automation isn't magic. Simply remember that you control the test execution through the scripts you create.

Selenium WebDriver

In TestWise, right-click a line between a test case (between it "...." do and end), and select "**Run ...**" (the ... is the test case name, for the example below, "*[1] User failed to sign in due to invalid password*")

```
 ⓣ 01_login_spec.rb  ✕                                                    ⌄
28                                                                        ⌃
21   ⊟   it "[1] Can sign in OK" do
22         puts("Go to login page")  ▶≣  Run "[1] Can sign in OK"       Ctrl+Shift+F9
23         goto_page("/login")
24         login_page = LoginPage.n  ▶   Run test cases in '01_login_spec'    Shift+F9
25         login_page.enter_usernam      Run Selected Scripts Against Current Browser   Alt+F11
26         login_page.enter_passwor
27         login_page.click_sign_in      Refactor                            >
28         # selenium does not have
29         sleep 0.6                     Run to line
30         try_for(3) { expect(driv
31         driver.find_element(:lin      Toggle Pausepoint              Ctrl+F9
32         puts "[stdout] Signed ou      Clear all Pausepoints
33       end
                                         ⌐ - -
```

A Chrome browser window will launch to run this login test.

> ## Best Practice
>
> **Run a test case and keep the browser open.**
>
> After test exeuction (pass or fail), you can inspect the page in Chrome, which is very helpful for debugging test script failures. For beginners, just remember this concept: after a test run, you may still want to interact with the app in that browser window.

Playwright

There are three options to running Playwright:

1. TestWise

Open the test project (`playwright/01-HelloPlaywright/hello-playwright.tpr`) in TestWise. Run the selected Playwright test in the same way as demonstrated earlier for Selenium tests.

2. Command line

Run the following command via command line in a terminal window.

```
cd 01-HelloPlaywright
npx playwright test --headed tests/launch_browser.spec.ts
```

3. Visual Studio Code

For how to set up PlayWright in Visual Studio Code, see the Appendix. To run individual tests, simply click the run button next to the test name, alternatively move the cursor to the test and use the shortcut Command + Semi-Colon, then C.

```
TS 04-login_ok.spec.ts          37   test('User can sign in OK', async () => {
TS 05-multi_login.spec.ts       38     await page.fill("#username", "agileway");
TS 07-login.spec.ts             39     await page.fill("#password", "testwise");
   agiletravelplaywright.tpr    40     await page.click("input:has-text('Sign in')");
   agiletravelplaywright.tws    41     const flashText = await page.locator("#flash_notice").textContent();
   buildwise.rake               42     expect(flashText).toContain('Signed in');
                                43   });
```

Figure 2. Appendix Run Test

Note that with running tests in Visual Studio Code, the browser is invisible (i.e. headless mode). Which is less fun! You'll certainly want to see your first test automation execution in action, so we recommend running the test via TestWise or commandline instead.

FAQ

1. Which Web Automation Framework is used in this book?

There are two covered in this book: Selenium WebDriver and Playwright.

- Selenium WebDriver

  Selenium complies with W3C's WebDriver standard, the only automation framework supported by all browser vendors (Google, Apple, Mozilla, and Microsoft).

- Playwright

  After a number of hyped and failed (deprecated or becoming so) frameworks in the JavaScript community, such as PhantomJS, Protractor, TestCafe and Cypress; Playwright is the current the favourite among JS testers.

However, all web automation frameworks do the same thing: driving the web apps based on W3C technologies (HTML, CSS, ...). So, for learning purposes, this book's content applies to all web automation frameworks.

2. Which scripting language for Selenium WebDriver? Ruby.

Selenium offers official language bindings in five languages: Ruby, Java, Python, JavaScript, and C#. For beginners, Ruby is the easiest to learn (and enjoyable for professionals). Once you master one language, switching to another is simple, as the Selenium syntax is consistent across all languages.

Zhimin's Selenium Recipes Book series covers all these five languages. We chose Ruby because it is an easy-to-learn yet powerful *scripting* language.

3. Which scripting language for Playwright? TypeScript.

Playwright, the other web automation framework we will cover in this book, has four language bindings: JavaScript, Java, Python, and C#. Within JavaScript, there are also two flavours: TypeScript or pure JavaScript.

We won't go into the language debate in this book (they can all get the job done), as the Playwright syntax is pretty much the same (excluding the language specifics). The simple reason we are adoptinng TypeScript in this book is because it is the default choice in Playwright official documentation.

4. Which Testing Tool? TestWise or Others

As a software testing engineer, you have the freedom to choose any testing tool that maximizes your efficiency. Simply select the one that suits you best, but we encourage trying a few. The main focus should be on mastering the design and creation of high-quality automated test scripts through these exercises.

> "There's more than one way to skin a cat."

Zhimin uses TestWise, a next-gen functional testing IDE, for both Selenium and Playwright. Courtney uses TestWise for Selenium and Visual Studio Code for Playwright.

2: Web Test Automation Simplified

In this exercise, we'll explore the background of Web Test Automation. You've likely seen a preschooler browsing the web. In an overly simplified version, web automation is doing that too, but instead of humans navigating manually, it's done with scripts. We're not claiming that web test automation is easy, but rather that the concept itself is quite simple.

Let's begin by gaining a deeper understanding of the web from a professional perspective.

Learning Objectives

To understand:

- Basic web terms.
- A web page's content is HTML.
- A web page what we see is rendering of local HTML downloaded from the remote site.
- Style (CSS) set the look and feel of web controls.
- JavaScript adds dynamic parts to a web page.
- 'Console' and 'Styles' in Chrome Inspector.

Web Basics

Here is a simple web page in a Chrome browser window.

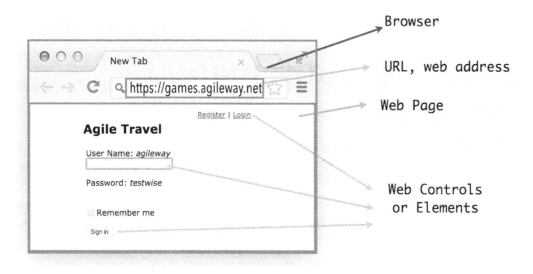

All terms, except one, should be familiar and make sense to everyone. A Uniform Resource Locator (URL) is the official term for a web address.

Web Testing means ...

Web testing, whether manual or automated, ensures that business features on a website are functioning correctly. A test case verifies a business feature (from GUI, i.e., browser) that involves one or more web pages.

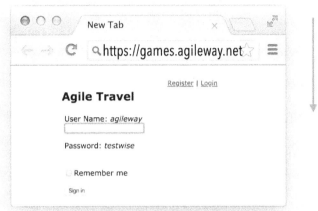

1. Find Element

2. Drive it

3. Check/Verify

Think about the steps for a user login test.

Web Test Automation means ...

Test Automation means automated scripts, not human beings, executing the test. Web Test Automation: use automated test scripts to drive controls in the browser (e.g. Chrome) to perform testing. *(Refer to the video demonstration in the last chapter)*

Manual testers will be pleased to know that the test design for manual testing largely applies to test automation as well. You simply need to "translate" the manual steps into automated ones. While there will be some differences, often with enhanced capabilities through automation, the overall test design remains quite similar between manual testing and web test automation.

For example, below are manual test steps for a user login test.

```
visit the test server https://whenwise.agileway.net
click the "SIGN IN" link on the top navigation bar
enter email "james@client.com"
enter password "test01"
click the "SIGN IN" button
wait a few seconds and expect the text "You have signed in successfully"
```

An equivalent raw Selenium WebDriver version:

```
driver.get "https://whenwise.agileway.net"
driver.find_element(:link, "SIGN IN").click
driver.find_element(:id, "email").send_keys("james@client.com")
driver.find_element(:name, "session[password]").send_keys("test01")
driver.find_element(:id, "login-btn").click
sleep 3
expect(page_text).to include("You have signed in successfully")
```

Or a refactored version based on Maintainable Automated Test Design.

```
driver.get "https://whenwise.agileway.net"
click_nav_sign_in
login_page = LoginPage.new(driver)
login_page.enter_email "james@client.com"
login_page.enter_password "test01"
login_page.click_sign_in
try_for(3) {
  expect(page_text).to include("You have signed in successfully")
}
```

Readers new to Selenium, don't worry about trying to understand every statement there, just to get an idea of automated test scripts that match the test design. By the way, you will learn to write this test, from scratch, in Exercise #04 (the raw Selenium version, the refactored version will be in Exercise #17), no prior experiences are required at all.

I want to just highlight one difference here. In automated scripts, we must provide every step with specifics, which is easy to understand. For example, "a few seconds" can be 3, 4, 5, or even 8. But in automated test script, we must set a specific number, in this case, 3 seconds.

How to Find an Element

To drive a control, we have to locate it first. It is very easy to do so. Right-click a control (a.k.a. element) in the Chrome browser and select "Inspect".

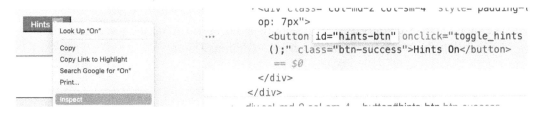

The browser window will show a panel (on the right). The text (as shown on the right in the above image) is the source of the web page, known as "Page Source". A web page source is in Hyper Text Markup Language (HTML).

Behind a web page is HTML

A web developer's main work is to create HTML pages, and web browsers (e.g. Chrome) render them to appear the way we see.

Hyper **T**ext **M**arkup **L**anguage

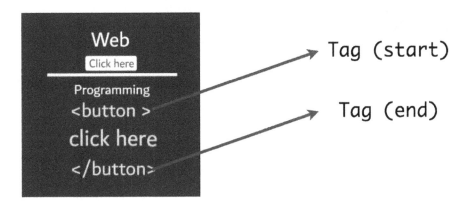

Tasks

Here are a few quick exercises to change a web page in your browser.

> Don't just read, do the exercises. The only practical way to master test automation is working on many hands-on exercises. — Zhimin Zhan

Task 1. Change Local Page Content (HTML)

Open https://games.agileway.net (a web address or URL) in Chrome.

> Zhimin: By the way, https://games.agileway.net hosts a game created by my son Dominic using JavaScript. As you might know, I'm against using JavaScript for end-to-end test automation (check the Resources section). However, I do know JavaScript well and use it when appropriate. My son wrote about 20 automated tests for this game, of course using Selenium Ruby — the same style of automated test scripts I've been using since 2011. I call it the "AgileWay Test Automation Formula," and the technologies are 100% free and open.
>
> Also, if you enjoy this game, please leave a note and I'll be sure to pass it on to my son to cheer him up!

Right-click the text 'Liney' and select 'Inspect'. You can see the "" tag is highlighted in the right panel.

Liney 1.0.4

```
solute;  margin
ize: 14x;">1.0.
<h3>Liney</h3>
```

Double-click the text Liney in the right panel.

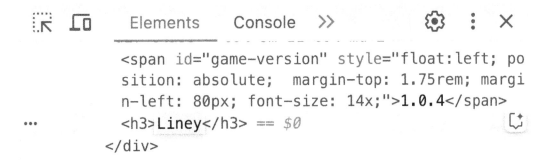

Change it to another word, such as "Mario". You changed the name on the web page as below:

Don't worry about it. You only changed the local web page in your browser. Refresh the page, and the original content will be back.

Task 2: Show/hide the Hints button (JavaScript)

JavaScript adds dynamic to web pages. Let's do a quick exercise, still on this Liney game site. There is a "Hints On" button.

Right-click anywhere on the page and select "Inspect". Click the "Console" tab. Try the following command in the console followed by the "Enter" key.

```
$("#hints-btn").hide();
```

The button disappeared. Run the show command (in the console) to bring it back.

```
$("#hints-btn").show();
```

Or toggle with a delay effect.

```
$("#hints-btn").toggle(2000);
```

2000 means 2 seconds (2000 milliseconds).

Task 3. Change the reload button style (CSS)

CSS (Cascading Style Sheets) adds styles to web pages. In this exercise, we will change the button's style (background and forward) in your local version of the web page.

1. Inspect the reload button, a yellow background one.

Right-click the button and select "Inspect" in Chrome.

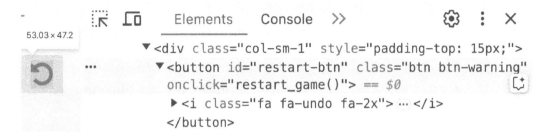

2. **Select the highlighted "" tag, then click the Styles panel at the bottom.**

```
▼<div class="col-sm-1" style="padding-top: 15px;">
   ▼<button id="restart-btn" class="btn btn-warning"
     onclick="restart_game()"> == $0
      ▶<i class="fa fa-undo fa-2x"> ··· </i>
   </button>
 </div>
```

◀ div.row   div.col-sm-1   **button#restart-btn.btn.btn-warning**   ▶

Styles   Computed   Layout   Event Listeners   ≫

🔽 Filter   :hov .cls +, 🎨 ▶|

```
element.style {
   : ;
}
```

—

0.800

ding   6

A beginner might need to try a few times to get into style editing mode.

3. **Enter a new style "background-color: red".**

4. Select `<i>` tag under the button', add style "color: blue".

The colors of the reload button have completely changed. Please feel free to explore more as well.

Summary

- A web developer creates a web page in HTML.

- A UI designer adds style sheets (CSS).
- A web developer makes it dynamic (JavaScript).
- A Browser renders HTML, CSS, and JS to a web page we see (many controls).
- Software testers execute tests to make sure web site works correctly.
- Web Test Automation Engineers write scripts to drive controls in the browser to perform testing.

3: Introduction to Web Automation Frameworks

Web automation tools (such as Selenium WebDriver and Playwright) are used to interact with and control web applications in a browser. In the software testing community, the term "framework" is used rather loosely. Here, we'll share our perspective on what constitutes an effective web automation framework:

- **Free** (as in freedom), preferably open-source.

  Micro Focus' Unified Functional Testing software (formerly known as QTP), once the industry-leading test automation tool, does not meet this criterion as you cannot run tests outside the proprietary tool and has since fallen out of favor.

  > "Free software is a matter of liberty, not price." - GNU Homepage[1]

- **Highly reliable**.

  Obviously, being intended for testing, execution reliability and support is crucial. Some hyped automation frameworks have quickly faded due to their lack of execution reliability and poor support.

- **No limitations**.

  Web technologies, as defined by the W3C, have seen minimal changes over the past 20 years (with HTML 4 released in 1998 and HTML 5 in 2014). Any "automation framework" must be capable of interacting with all web page elements conforming to W3C standards. If a web automation framework is

---

[1]https://www.gnu.org

unable to handle certain controls, such as frames, shadow DOMs, or tabs, it limits the ability to automate test scenarios involving those elements. Cypress, for instance, falls short in this regard.

- **Well supported**, especially by browser vendors.

  Web automation tests run within web browsers, which are updated frequently—about every two months for Google Chrome and monthly for Firefox. Some older commercial test automation tools have become obsolete because they could not keep pace with browser updates and other related web technoglgies.

Learning Objectives

- Basic Selenium WebDriver/Playwright syntax
- Three Simple Selenium locators: ID, NAME, LINK
- Two Simple Playwright locators: ID, CSS
- Try out automated test steps
- TestWise's debugging mode (*a fast way to try out selenium steps*)

Selenium WebDriver

Selenium WebDriver is a widely-used open-source framework for automating web browser interactions, built on the WebDriver standard defined by the W3C. This standard ensures consistent behavior and compatibility across modern browsers.

Selenium WebDriver's intuitive syntax pattern

Selenium WebDriver is the easiest-to-learn automation framework because its syntax follows such a simple and intuitive pattern.

One simple pattern: locate a web control and drive it

Step 1. **Find** a control (element)
by one of 8 locators

Step 2. **Act** on it

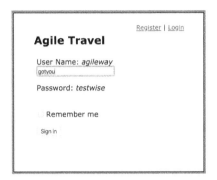

Step 1. Locate the control

Right-click a web control, e.g. a text field or link, in Chrome and select "Inspect".

The HTML (introduced in Ex#02) for the selected control is highlighted on the right panel. In this example (above), the HTML for the user name text field (for users to enter a username) is

```
<input type="text" name="user_name" id="username" size="25">
```

Beginners might worry about the above HTML syntax as they think they are not web developers. Please don't worry. The HTML knowledge required by test automation engineers is actually quite limited.

Step 2. Perform action on the located control

After locating a web control, what will be next? Perform an action on it, logically. Think about what you can do with common web elements:

- **Link**: Click it.

- **Text Field**: Type text in it.

How will they be done in Selenium?

1. **Click on a link**

   ```
   driver.find_element(:link, "Login").click
   ```

2. **Send keys to (Type in) a text field**

   ```
   driver.find_element(:id, "username").send_keys("agileway")
   ```

The Selenium syntax is quite intuitive, isn't it?

> Note: some readers might think `type` (in *Cypress*) or `fill` (in *Playwright*) more intuitive as an action for a text box. Wrong! You can "fill" a textbox with a piece of text, but would you say `fill` to send an `Enter` or `Up` key? Therefore, `send_keys` is accurate, `type` and `fill` are not.

After all, WebDriver syntax was created by W3C experts after many rounds of review (took years). In contrast, Cypress launched its version 1 without support for Frames— a feature that has been standard for over a decade and remains widely used in many enterprise applications. Such a limitation reflects, at best, a lack of professionalism.

Common Controls on a web page

There are a fixed set of web controls on a standard web page, and you are familiar with most of those and have used them already, such as:

- **Link** (a.k.a. hyperlink)
  Click to navigate to another web page.

- **Text field** (a.k.a. text box)

  For users to enter text.

- **Check box**

  Yes or No option.

- **Radio button**

  To choose one from a small set of pre-defined options.

- **Button**

  To perform an action, for example, submitting a form.

- **Drop-down list** (a.k.a. select list)

  To choose one or more options from a pre-defined list.

- **Information controls**

  For users to read, not act on. e.g. text on the page.

  - `h2`, heading 2 *(there are also h1, h3, ...)*
  - `label`, `div'`, `span`
  - `p`, a paragraph

There are a few more types, in the context of Web Automation, but they are not much different. It mostly boils down to the categories above.

Selenium WebDriver's Locators

After understanding the controls (a.k.a. elements) on a web page, we will learn how to locate a specific element in Selenium. Do you still remember Selenium's pattern: **"Locate a web control, then drive it"**?

The way to locate an element in Selenium is to use one of its eight locators. Let's start with three simple ones.

ID Locator

The HTML for the user name text field is

```
<input type="text" name="user_name" id="username">
```

The ID for this element is username. Below is a Selenium statement using ID locator.

```
driver.find_element(:id, "username")
```

You may have some questions. For now, you just need to know that we can use "ID" (in HTML) to locate a specific web control.

Name Locator

Besides ID, we commonly use the element's NAME attribute to identify an element.

```
<input type="text" name="user_name" id="username">
```

For the same control (user name text field), the below works too.

```
driver.find_element(:name, "user_name")
```

Link Text Locator

This one is easy to understand: locating a hyperlink based on the displayed link text.

```
driver.find_element(:link_text, "Login")
```

You can also use the shorter :link syntax, e.g. `driver.find_element(:link, "Login")`.

We have covered 3 out of 8 Selenium locators now. They are quite easy, aren't they? We will introduce the remaining locators later.

Run Selenium Scripts in TestWise

Now, let's run the above Selenium scripts in TestWise.

In a typical one-on-one coaching session, Zhimin would have had TestWise ready for the attendees to try out the scripts (*Apple calls them Playgrounds*). If you haven't installed TestWise yet, check out Ex01. It only takes about one minute to install the TestWise Ruby edition on Windows.

For readers using macOS or Linux, after Ruby & gems & chromedriver, install TestWise standard edition. It is not complex either.

If you choose not to use TestWise, that's perfectly fine. All test scripts in this workbook are built on completely free and open-source frameworks and can be executed directly from the command line. You can continue the exercises with your preferred test tool, though some content may not be applicable. In such cases, focus on completing the test cases and applying the design and debugging practices using your chosen tool.

Get TestWise in Playgrounds mode

1. **Launch TestWise**

   For installation of TestWise, see Ex#01.

2. **Open the sample test project in TestWise**

   Click the "(raw Selenium)" link in the TestWise's start page.

3. **Open a sample RSpec test script**

   Click 01_login_spec.rb (on the left) to open it.

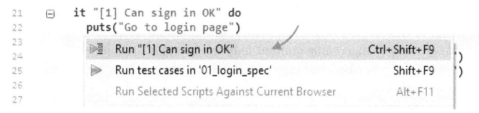

4. Run an individual test case

Right-click line 23 and select "Run [1] Can sign in OK" test case. (*In fact, any line between under it "[1]...." will do*).

```
21    ⊟    it "[1] Can sign in OK" do
22             puts("Go to login page")
23
24    ▶▤  Run "[1] Can sign in OK"                       Ctrl+Shift+F9    )
25    ▷   Run test cases in '01_login_spec'             Shift+F9         )
26        Run Selected Scripts Against Current Browser   Alt+F11
27
```

A Chrome browser window will launch. After test execution, this browser would remain open.

5. Select one test step and run it against the lastly opened browser window (TestWise)

Select the line `driver.navigate.to(site_url + "/login")`, right-click and select "Run Selected Scripts Against Current Browser".

```
21  ⊟  it "[1] Can sign in OK" do
22        puts("Go to login page")
23      | driver.navigate.to(site_url + "/login") ▶▤  Run "[1] Can sign in OK"                        Ctrl+Shift+F9
24        driver.find_element(:id, "username").sen
25        driver.find_element(:id, "password").sen ▷  Run test cases in '01_login_spec'              Shift+F9
26        driver.find_element(:id, "username").sub   Run Selected Scripts Against Current Browser    Alt+F11
27
```

You will see that TestWise opens a new file (if it does not exists already): `debugging_spec.rb`. The test step is copied over this special test script.

```
 (T) 01_login_spec.rb  X      debugging_spec.rb  X
  1        # Special test that uses last browser window (from a TestWise run)
  2        # Then you can try Selenium commands directly on the page, without
  3
  4        load File.dirname(__FILE__) + "/../test_helper.rb"
  5
  6      describe "DEBUG" do
  7         include TestHelper
  8
  9         before(:all) do
 10            use_current_browser
 11         end
 12
 13         it "Debugging" do
 14            driver.navigate.to(site_url + "/login")
 15         end
 16      end
```

If you pay attention, that step (and only that step) has been just executed in the open browser window.

6. **In TestWise's "debugging mode"**

The last step enters the so-called "TestWise Debugging Mode". The "debugging mode" in Testing is different from the programmer's way of using debuggers. It is far simpler. In TestWise, it is a "Playgrounds" mode to try out automated scripts.

Important note: the Chrome browser window must be kept open.

Try out automated test steps

Change the test steps, between it "Debugging" do and end, to try clicking the Register link. Then run this test script.

```
it "Debugging" do
  driver.find_element(:link, "Register").click
end
```

Click the blue triangle button on the toolbar to run it.

01_login_spec.rb ✕   debugging_spec.rb ✕

You will notice that the page in the Chrome browser window changed, i.e., the 'Register' link is clicked.

Type another step to click the Login link.

```ruby
it "Debugging" do
  driver.find_element(:link, "Register").click
  driver.find_element(:link, "Login").click
end
```

Run it again.

Tip: I suggest moving the Chrome window and TestWise side by side, make the window smaller if you have to.

Astute readers might notice that the "Register" link got clicked again. That is correct. How do I just click the "Login" link but not delete the "Register" line above?

Knowledge Point: Comment in code/scripts

The comments in code/scripts are ignored by computers but may help human beings (understand or keep statements that are temporarily not applicable).

Make one or more test steps as comments so that they won't be run.

To do that in Ruby: add the # in the front of the line.

```
it "Debugging" do
  # driver.find_element(:link, "Register").click
  driver.find_element(:link, "Login").click
end
```

Try it out.

The page shown in the browser shall be the Login page.

Let's fill in a user name.

```
it "Debugging" do
  # driver.find_element(:link, "Register").click
  driver.find_element(:link, "Login").click
  driver.find_element(:id, "username").send_keys("agileway")
end
```

Run the above in TestWise "debugging mode" (again). The text was entered in the textbox.

Please feel free to try more, such as:

- Enter another username
- Enter a password
- Click another link

Playwright

Playwright, developed by Microsoft, is a web automation framework similar in functionality to Selenium WebDriver. Here is the equivalent 'User Login Test' in Playwright (*compare this with the Selenium version from the previous exercise*).

```
test('User can sign in OK', async () => {
  // await page.locator('text=Register').click();
  await page.locator('text=Login').click();
  await page.fill("#username", "agileway");
});
```

Some people claim that Playwright syntax is better than Selenium. We disagree for two reasons:

1. Lacking a consistent syntax pattern.
2. We can achieve more concise and end-user friendly top-level script using Page Object Model, so the language syntax itself matters less (*will be covered in later chapters*)

Anyway, you can run Playwright tests in TestWise.

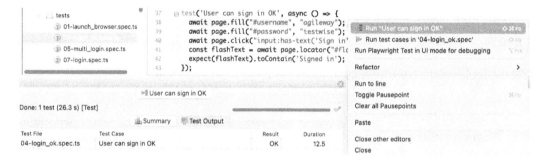

Figure 3. Execute the test case in TestWise macOS edition

However, TestWise does not offer a "Debugging Mode" for Playwright test execution. The reason for this is that Zhimin invented the "Attaching to Browser" debugging mode and implemented it in TestWise for Selenium + RSpec & Selenium + Pytest, leveraging the openness of the RSpec & Pytest syntax framework. In contrast, Playwright's test runner is less open, which limits similar capabilities.

FAQ

- **What are the differences, in terms of execution, between TestWise's debugging and normal mode?**

In TestWise's debugging mode, you don't need to launch a new browser window. You will continue with the lastly opened browser window. There are many benefits of doing that. For now, you have surely noticed one: it is faster!

- **Can I manually navigate to another site (or page) and then continue running new/existing test steps in TestWise debugging mode?**

  Yes, as long as TestWise is still attached to the chrome window. Note, TestWise is only able to attach to the most recent Chrome Window launched by TestWise.

- **Can I use this debugging mode in Visual Studio Code or other tools?**

  Maybe. The technique is public (confident programmers can read the test_-helper.rb , Searching —remote_debugging_port). For more, check out my other article "My Innovative Solution to Test Automation: Attach test execution to the existing browser[2]".

  However, to our knowledge, there is no testing tool to support it as what TestWise does. By the way. Visual Studio Code is a powerful programmer's editor, not a testing tool. It is possible to develop an extension like TestWise's debugging mode though.

---

[2]https://agileway.substack.com/p/my-innovative-solution-to-test-automation

4: User Sign in OK Test

For now on, we are going to work on test cases together. Let's start with a simple one: "User sign in OK". As a matter of fact, testing user login is usually the first testing task for an app.

Exercise #04

Test Case 04

User can login AgileTravel site with valid user name and password.

Test Data
    Site URL: http://travel.agileway.net
    User Login/Password: agileway/testwise

Test Steps
    Go to URL
    Enter username "agileway"
    Enter password "testwise"
    Click button "Sign In"
    Verify: "Signed in!"

While I believe everyone understands the steps, we still ask you to perform the manual testing (exact steps) first.

"Before starting scripting an automated test, always perform manual testing first. Many beginners forget about this, too eager to jump directly into scripting." — Zhimin Zhan

Learning Objectives

- Create a test project in TestWise
- Create a test case
- Validate
- Execute a single test case

Tasks

Create a test project in TestWise (introduced in Ex#01), then script the test steps one by one in TestWise debugging mode (introduced in Ex#03). After all the steps pass, move all of them into a test script file.

Selenium WebDriver

Task 1. Create a new TestWise Project (Selenium + RSpec)

A project in coding/scripting is a folder that contains all related files for one purpose.

Launch TestWise and create a new project (File → New Project). If a project is already opened, close it first (File → Close Project).

Fill in the pop-up window with appropriate details, as below.

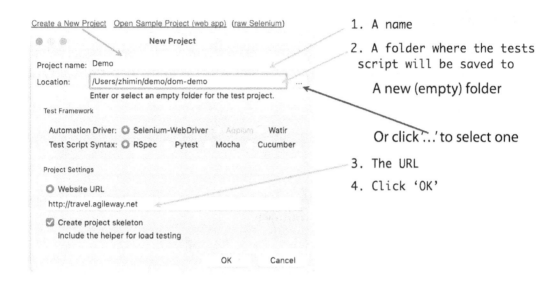

- **The Project Name**

  Can be any text for identification purposes.

- **The Project Location**

  A project folder where the test scripts and related files are stored. We suggest you create an empty folder and type (or paste) its full path there, e.g.

    - Windows: `C:\Users\me\demo\my-first-test-project`
    - macOS: `/Users/me/demo/my-first-test-project`
    - Linux: `/home/me/demo/my-first-test-project`

   Tip: don't include space, special characters or unicode characters (e.g. emojis) in the folder path.

- **The target server URL**

  From our test task card, http://travel.agileway.net.

Click the "OK" button to create the project. TestWise will open this newly-created project with a set of files.

Task 2. Create Login Test

In TestWise, click new_spec.rb (on the left) to open it and run the test case as below. Yes, it is an empty test case, the purpose of doing this is to get into the TestWise Debugging Mode.

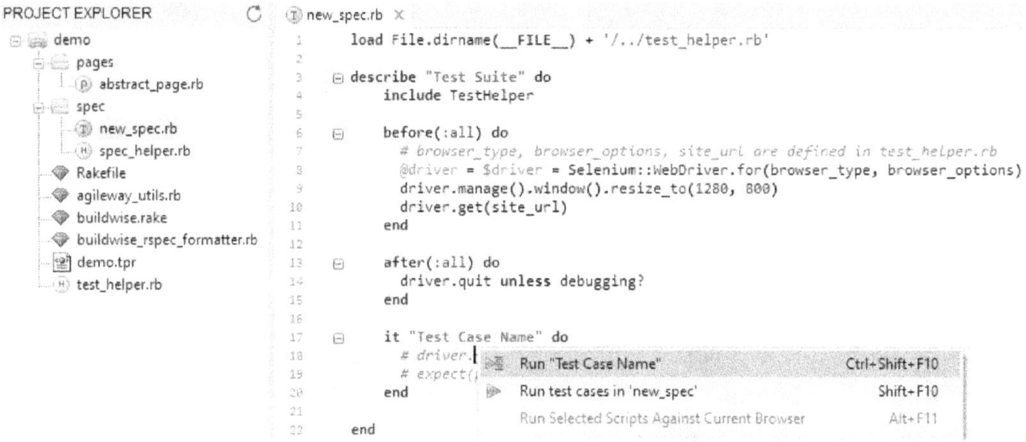

Figure 4. Right-click a line between and select (the first item)

A Chrome browser window will launch and open our target website. If you don't get this, then your test execution environment is not correct, see the FAQ.

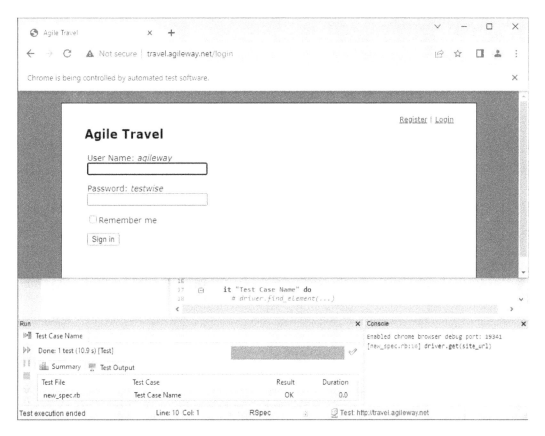

Highlight one commented line (e.g. 18), and select the `Run Selected Scripts Against Current Browser` (the third option) to enter *TestWise Debugging mode*.

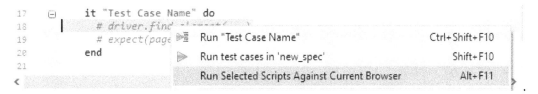

Task 3. Scripting automation steps

Check out the test task card. There are four action steps:

1. Open the server URL (done).
2. Enter username "agileway".

3. Enter password "testwise".
4. Click the button "Sign in".

Let's do steps 2 — 4 one by one.

Step 1. Open the target website in a browser

The skeleton test script, created the project creation by TestWise, includes this step: opening the target site URL.

```
@driver = Selenium::WebDriver.for(browser_type, browser_options)
driver.get(site_url)  # site_url is defined as "https://travel.agileway.net"
```

Step 2. Enter the user name "agileway"

Right-click the user name text box (in the existing Chrome browser), and select "Inspect".

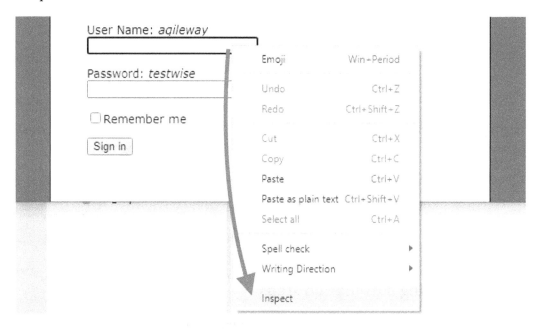

Make the browser bigger enough to see both the page and its source (on the right).

The HTML for the user name text box:

```
<input type="text" name="username" id="username" size="25">
```

We can use its ID to locate it. Add the following test script statements in debugging_-spec.rb and run the test (by clicking the blue play button on the toolbar).

```
driver.find_element(:id, "username").send_keys("agileway")
```

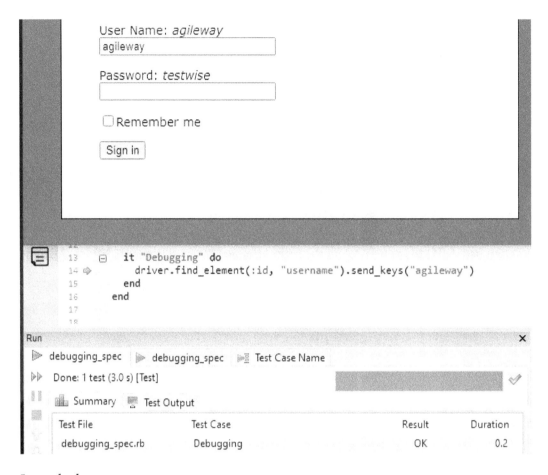

It worked.

Step 3. Enter the password "testwise"

Comment out (type # in the front) the above test step in debugging_spec.rb and continue to work out the next step in the same manner.

The HTML for this password text box:

```
<input id="password" name="password" type="password" size="25">
```

We can use its ID like the previous step. I recommend trying the NAME locator just to practice. The test step will be:

```
# driver.find_element(:id, "username").send_keys("agileway")
driver.find_element(:name, "password").send_keys("testwise")
```

Run the step in debugging mode.

Step 4. Click the "Sign in" button

Repeat the same process as you have done before:

- Comment out the previous test steps.
- Inspect the new control (in this case, a button)
- Find out its HTML.

```
<input type="submit" name="commit" value="Sign in">
```

- Write the test statement.

```
driver.find_element(:name, "commit").click
```

- Run it in the debugging mode.

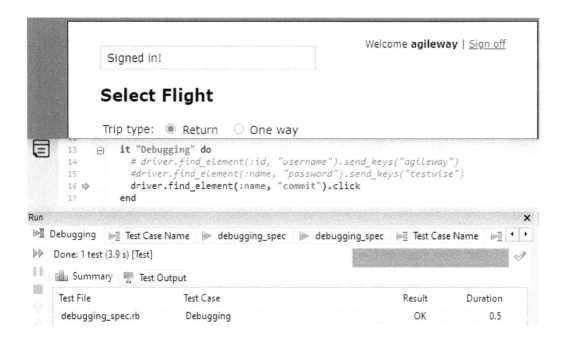

So far we have tried out the test steps in `debugging_spec.rb` (TestWise debugging mode). Now we know these three test steps are working.

Task 4. Copy the working test steps over to the test script file

Copy them over to the test script file `new_spec.rb`. Remove all leading # characters (comments).

```
spec                          16
  new_spec.rb                 17  ⊟  it "Test Case Name" do
  spec_helper.rb              18        driver.find_element(:id, "username").send_keys("agileway")
  debugging_spec.rb           19        driver.find_element(:name, "password").send_keys("testwise")
  Rakefile                    20        driver.find_element(:name, "commit").click
                              21      end
```

Run the test case (please note, this is not in debugging mode).

```
17    ⊟  it "Test Case Name" do
18         driver.
19         driver.    ▷̄  Run "Test Case Name"                    Ctrl+Shift+F10
20         driver.    ▷   Run test cases in 'new_spec'             Shift+F10
21       end
              Run Selected Scripts Against Current Browser         Alt+F11
```

You will see a new Chrome browser launch and run those test steps to log in to the site successfully.

Step 5. Add an assertion

A test is incomplete without assertions (a.k.a checks). For this simple login test, how do you verify a successful login? Some might say *"It is obvious, we are signed in"*. However, in automated test scripts, assertions have to be specific. For example, the "Signed in!" text is found on the page.

```
<div id="flash_notice">Signed in!</div>
```

The assertion step will be:

```
expect(page_text).to include("Signed in")
```

A more precise assertion is to check the exact match against the text in a specific HTML element.

```
expect(drive.find_element(:id, "flash_notice").text).to eq("Signed in!")
```

Task 6. Change the test case name and test script file

So far, the test script steps have been saved in new_spec.rb, the sample file created by TestWise.

1. **Change test case name**

   Change it "Test Case Name" to it "User can sign in OK".

2. **Change the test script file**

   Click the X shape icon next to the file name (as indicated below) to close the new_spec.rb.

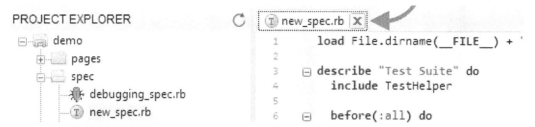

Right-click the file new_spec.rb in the "Project Explorer", and select "**Rename**".

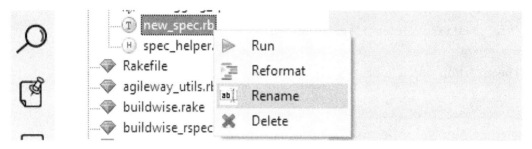

Type a new name, such as login_spec.rb.

Run the test case in login_spec.rb to make sure it is still running fine.

Playwright

Task 1. Create a new TestWise Project (Playwright Test)

Run `npm install` from the command line in the project folder, in this case, `demo/04-Login`.

Task 2. Create Login Test

Rename the `new.spec.ts` to `login.spec.ts`, and change the test name, from `test('Case Name', async ...` to `test('User can log in', async ...`. Run it.

Task 3. Scripting test steps

- **Open the site URL**.

   This is also created by TestWise (if you are using it).

```
test.beforeEach(async () => {
  await page.goto(Helper.site_url());
});
```

- **Enter username "agileway".**

According to Playwright documentation[1], "Using locator.fill() is the easiest way to fill out the form fields".

Playwright ID locator is a straightforward and efficient way to target web elements based on their unique id attribute.

```
await page.locator('#username').fill("agileway");
```

There is a simpler syntax. However, Playwright recommends the locator syntax. We will use both in this book where we can to show both are acceptable.

```
await page.fill("#username", "agileway");
```

- **Enter password "testwise".**

```
await page.fill("#password", "testwise");
```

> In Playwright documentation[2], await page.getByLabel('Password').fill('secret'), works for the HTML like the below.
>
> ```
> <label>Password <input type="password" /></label>
> ```
>
> But that Playwright statement depends on the label HTML element around the input element. In this case, it does not work for the AgileTravel site which does not use labels like that.

- **Click the button "Sign in".**

We can use CSS locator[3] for this operation.

---

[1]https://playwright.dev/docs/input#text-input
[2]https://playwright.dev/docs/locators#locate-by-label
[3]https://playwright.dev/docs/other-locators#css-locator

```
await page.locator("input:has-text('Sign in')").click();
```

Or, the equivalent to the above:

```
await page.click("input:has-text('Sign in')");
```

Task 5. Add an assertion

In Playwright, `textContent()` retrieves the text of a specific element, commonly used for assertions.

```
const flashText = await page.textContent("#flash_notice")
expect(flashText).toEqual('Signed in!');
```

or

```
const flashText = await page.locator("#flash_notice").textContent();
expect(flashText).toEqual('Signed in!');
```

Full Test Script

Selenium WebDriver

```ruby
load File.dirname(__FILE__) + "/../test_helper.rb"
describe "Test Suite" do
  include TestHelper  before(:all) do
    # browser_type, site_url defined in test_helper.rb
    @driver = Selenium::WebDriver.for(browser_type, browser_options)
    driver.manage().window().resize_to(1280, 800)
    driver.get(site_url)
  end

  after(:all) do
    driver.quit unless debugging?
  end
```

```
  it "User can sign in OK" do
    driver.find_element(:id, "username").send_keys("agileway")
    driver.find_element(:name, "password").send_keys("testwise")
    driver.find_element(:name, "commit").click
    expect(page_text).to include("Signed in!")
  end
end
```

Playwright

```
import { test, Page, expect } from '@playwright/test';
var path = require("path");

test.describe.configure({ mode: 'serial' });

import * as Helper from '../test_helper.js'

//Reuse the page among the test cases in the test script file
let page: Page;

test.beforeAll(async ({ browser }) => {
  page = await browser.newPage();
});

test.afterAll(async () => {
   await page.close();
});

test.beforeEach(async () => {
  await page.goto(Helper.site_url());
});

test('User can sign in OK', async () => {
  await page.fill("#username", "agileway");
  await page.fill("#password", "testwise");
  await page.click("input:has-text('Sign in!')");
  const flashText = await page.textContent("#flash_notice")
```

```
    expect(flashText).toEqual('Signed in!');
});
```

Common Issues

- **Typing errors**

  Beginners often make typing errors in scripts (i.e., typos), which can prevent test cases from running. In the next scripting session, We will show you a way to detect syntax errors quickly.

- **Unable to remember Selenium/Playwright syntax**

  You don't have to remember it. We will show you a much quicker and more fun way to enter Selenium and Playwright statements in the next scripting session. In the meantime, just type it in based on the chapter.

FAQ

- **I am totally new to test automation, there are parts I don't quite follow**.

  If this is your first automated test script, don't be too hard on yourself. It's completely normal for beginners to feel frustrated over simple mistakes like typos.

  We suggest you watch this screencast (YouTube video[4]) and follow it step by step. If you still have specific questions, please feel leave a message on the book site or contacted us on . We will help. The key point is that you're about to step into the exciting world of web test automation, it would be a huge pity for something we didn't explain well in words.

  If you want to try a one-on-one coaching session, check out Zhimin's 30-minutes Test Automation Coaching for $1[5].

---

[4]https://youtu.be/-RU4NaXvJU8
[5]https://agileway.substack.com/p/30-minutes-test-automation-coaching

- There are some test statements (generated by TestWise), such as `Selenium::WebDriver.for(browser_type, browser_options)`. Can you explain them?

Don't worry about that for now—just focus on the goals of this exercise. Rest assured, all test scripts are written in plain text and are not dependent on any specific vendor or tool.

This exercise book is specifically designed for absolute beginners. Each session is purposefully crafted, and we'll explain the statements in detail when the time is right.

5: Multi-Login Tests

Building on from the previous exercise: one automated login test, this exercise will add one more login test case in the same test script file.

Exercise 05

It's quite common to have multiple test cases, such as using different test users, for user authentication.

Test Data

```
Site URL:             https://travel.agileway.net
Regular User Login:   'agileway' / 'testwise'
Admin   User Login:   'admin' / 'secret'
```

Learning Objectives

- Understand Test Syntax Frameworks.

- Learn RSpec test structure.
- `before(:all)`, `before(:each)`, `after(:each)`, `after(:all)` in RSpec.
- Learn @playwright/test structure.
- Navigate to a URL.
- Execute each test case individually.
- Execute all test cases in a test script file.

Test Design

We can build from the test script file from the previous exercise.

1. Copy the content of the existing login-ok test case.
2. Paste after the test case, change the test name to "Admin user sign in OK".
3. Update the test data in the entering username and password steps.

Essentially, there are two similar test cases, for each one:

1. Navigate to the login URL, `https://travel.agileway.net/login`.
2. Enter username, password, and click the sign-in button.
3. Assertion.

Knowledge Point: Automation + Test Syntax Frameworks

Software test professionals often say, 'We use the X test automation framework,' referring to examples like Selenium or Playwright. However, in reality, two distinct frameworks are involved.

Test Automation framework = Automation + Test Syntax

Selenium WebDriver and Playwright are web automation (also known as Driver) frameworks, which drives an app within a web browser.

Let's have a look at the test script we have done in the previous session.

RSpec Example: Selenium WebDriver

```
describe "User Authentication" do

  before(:all) do
    @driver = Selenium::WebDriver.for(:chrome)
    @driver.get("http://travel.agileway.net")
  end

  after(:all) do
    @driver.quit
  end

  it "[01] User can login" do
    driver.find_element(:id,"username").send_keys("agileway")
    driver.find_element(:name,"password").send_keys("testwise")
    driver.find_element(:xpath,"//input[@value='Sign In']").click
    expect(driver.page_source).to include("Login OK!")
  end

  it "[02] Deny access for invalid password" do
    # Next Story Test
  end
end
```

Story ID: TestCase

Operations

Assertion

Besides the opening the target site *(in* `before(:all)`*)*, there are three driving-control statements (*indicated by arrows*), matching the test design.

Best Practice: One Statement for One Step in Design

As shown in the test scripts above, each test step corresponds to a single user operation (*not 100% of the time, but close*). This design offers many benefits, but we'll focus on just one here: it simplifies test design. Don't you agree?

What is a **test syntax framework** then? A Test Syntax Framework provides:

- **Syntax Structure**

  Such as it "a test case" do marks the start of one test case for Rspec.

- **Assertions**

  A test is not complete without checks (a.k.a assertions). expect(...).to include("...") is an assertion.

- **Test reporting**

  Capturing the test results.

The test syntax framework you have seen is **RSpec**. RSpec is a Behaviour Driven Development (BDD) framework in Ruby language.

rspec 3.8.0

BDD for Ruby

◯ Star   2,861

TOTAL DOWNLOADS
803,908,173

FOR THIS VERSION
211,198,983

Figure 5. RSpec 3.8.0 has over 200 million downloads

Warning: Avoid Cucumber   and   other   Gherkin   BDD frameworks

If you have never heard of "Cucumber" or "Gherkin", good; as they are bad for test automation. Then you can safely ignore this section.

This section is for readers who have heard of "Cucumber" and "Gherkin". Be aware of Cucumber and its variants such as SpecFlow and Concordion, and those "Given, Then, When" (i.e. Gherkin) style test frameworks.

Automated tests in a Gherkin framework are often appealing to managers and business analysts, great for demonstrations. But in reality, to my knowledge, all test automation attempts using Gherkin have failed badly. Some might think that's me being subjective, but "Cucumber as a test tool it sucks" is actually the comment from Cucumber's creator. For more, check out some of my articles:

- Why Gherkin (Cucumber, SpecFlow,...) Always Failed with UI Test Automation?[1] *(featured in Medium's top publication: The Startup)*
- A Practical Advice on Rejecting Gherkin for Test Automation[2]

To summarise, avoid Cucumber, and avoid "Given, When, Then" in automated test scripts. Just use RSpec.

Learn RSpec in under a minute

RSpec is simple and easier to learn.

- **Test Group**: `describe "a group of related test cases" do` to its matching end

  A test group can contain one or more test cases.

  Example: `describe("User Authentication")` in "login_spec.rb", a test script file may contain several test cases.

- **Test Case**: `it "one test case" do` to its matching end

  For a test case, you can use plain English as the test case name.

  Examples: `it "User login OK" do`, `it "User login failed" do`.

---

[1] https://agileway.substack.com/p/why-gherkin-cucumber-specflow-always
[2] https://agileway.substack.com/p/a-practical-advice-on-rejecting-gherkin

- **Expectation**: `expect(actual).to match(exepcted)`

  i.e. Assertion.

  Example: `expect(page_text).to include("Sign in successful")`

Of course, RSpec offers many more features, but a basic understanding of RSpec is sufficient for functional automated testing.

Before and After test case sections in RSpec

Have a look at a complete Rspec test structure (on the left).

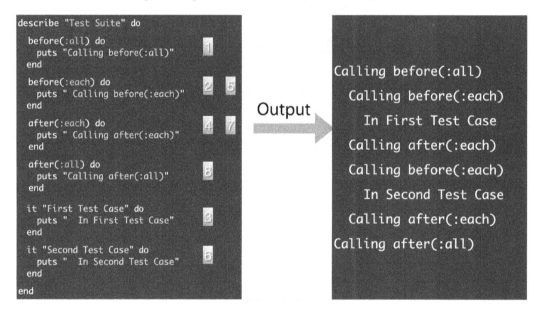

Besides `describe` and `it` (*two of them*), there are `before(:all)`, `before(:each)`, `after(:each)` and `after(:all)`. These are called hooks which are used to execute scripts before and after test cases.

Now, try to work out the output of the RSpec test on the left. The purpose of this simple exercise is to understand the execution order. Compare yours with the answer (on the right).

The test syntax framework in @playwright/test

The npm package we used is named @playwright/test, which includes the test syntax framework. Due to the success of RSpec, many other test syntax frameworks in different languages have adopted a similar syntax.

@playwright/test sytnax and structure

- **Test Group**:

```
test.describe('Example Group', () => {
  test('one', async ({ page }) => {
    // ...
  });

  test('two', async ({ page }) => {
    // ...
  });
});
```

The test group is optional in @playwright/test. In fact, we like the form without it, but you are free to make your own choice.

- **Test Case**

```
test('Regular User Sign in OK', async () => {
  // ...
});

 
```

- **Before and After test case sections**

```
test.beforeAll(async ({ browser }) => {
  page = await browser.newPage();      // Create page once.
});

test.afterAll(async () => {
   await page.close();   // Close it
});

test.beforeEach(async () => {
  // ...
});

test.afterEach(async () => {
  // ...
});
```

- **Assertions**

   Example:

```
const content = await page.textContent('h1');
expect(content).toBe('WhenWise')
```

See, it is quite similar to RSpec, right?

Variations of @playwright/test syntax

Unlike RSpec, which follows a consistent format, @playwright/test has some variations (which JavaScript engineers will likely not find surprising). You can find more on this Playwright doc[3], such as `test.describe.fixme`, `test.describe.only`, `test.describe.skip`, `test.extend`, `test.fixme`, `test.only`, `test.setTimeout`, `test.skip`, `test.slow`, `test.step`, ..., etc.

However, we do not recommend spending too much time on those test syntax framework features. Zhimin has successfully developed many test automation projects over the past 15 years using only the basic RSpec knowledge shown above.

---

[3](https://playwright.dev/docs/api/class-test)

Tasks

Selenium WebDriver + RSpec

Task 1. Navigate to a URL

```
driver.get("https://...")
```

Below is equivalent to the above.

```
driver.navigate.to("https://...")
```

Task 2. Execute test script file (multiple test cases)

In previous sessions, we have shown running an individual test case in TestWise (as shown below).

```
it "Admin User sign in OK" do
  driver.find_element(:id, "username").send_keys("admin")
  driver.find_element(:name, "password").send_keys("secret")
  driver.find_element(:name, "commit").click |      ▶≣ Run "Admin User sign in OK"         ⇧ ⌘ F9
  expect(driver.find_element(:id, "flash_notic       ▶ Run test cases in '05-multi_login_spec'    ⇧ F9
end                                                    Run Selected Scripts Against Current Browser  ⌥ F11
```

To run the script file (i.e. all test cases in the test script file), you can select the second menu option (*Run test cases in 'test script file name'*),

```
it "User Sign in OK" do
  driver.find_element(:id, "username").send_keys("agileway")
  driver.find_element(:name, "password").send_keys("testwise")
  driver.find_element(:name, "commit").click    ▶≣ Run "User Sign in OK"                   ⇧ ⌘ F9
  expect(driver.find_element(:id, "flash_notic     ▶ Run test cases in '05-multi_login_spec'    ⇧ F9
end                                                  Run Selected Scripts Against Current Browser  ⌥ F11

it "Admin User sign in OK" do                      Refactor                                       >
  driver.find_element(:id, "username").send_ke
  driver.find_element(:name, "password").send_     Run to line
  driver.find_element(:name, "commit").click       Toggle Pausepoint                           ⌘ F8
  expect(driver.find_element(:id, "flash_notic     Clear all Pausepoints
end
```

or click the blue play button on the toolbar.

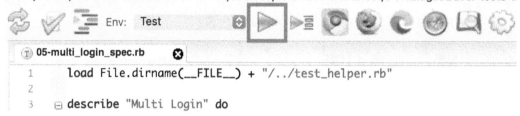

The run results panel in TestWise shows the results of two test cases.

Test File	Test Case	Result	Duration
05-multi_login_spec.rb	User Sign in OK	OK	3.1
05-multi_login_spec.rb	Admin User sign in OK	Failed	0.5

Figure 6. The output (in TestWise) after executing one single RSpec test script, containing two test cases.

There's a test execution failure, but don't worry—this is the expected outcome for this exercise. Run the three test executions as outlined below:

- First test case: PASS
- Second test case: PASS
- Entire test script file (with both test cases): FAILED

The reasons for this will be explained in the next two exercises. The goal here is to demonstrate the difference between executing individual test cases and running multiple test cases within a single test script file.

Task 3. Optimize the test scripts to use `before(:each)` hook

For the following two test cases, do you notice their first test step is the same?

```
it "Login test 1" do
  driver.get("https://travel.agileway.net")
  driver.find_element(:id, "username").send_keys("agileway")
  driver.find_element(:name, "password").send_keys("testwise")
  driver.find_element(:name, "commit").click
end

it "Login test 2" do
  driver.get("https://travel.agileway.net")
  driver.find_element(:id, "username").send_keys("admin")
  driver.find_element(:name, "password").send_keys("secret")
  driver.find_element(:name, "commit").click
end
```

In other words, this step runs before each test case. We can move it to the
before(:each) hook.

```
before(:each) do
  driver.get("https://travel.agileway.net")
end

it "Login test 1" do
  driver.find_element(:id, "username").send_keys("agileway")
  # ...
end

it "Login test 2" do
  driver.find_element(:id, "username").send_keys("admin")
  # ...
end
```

Full Test Script (Selenium RSpec)

```
load File.dirname(__FILE__) + "/../test_helper.rb"

describe "Multi Login" do
  include TestHelper

  before(:all) do
    @driver = Selenium::WebDriver.for(browser_type, browser_options)
    driver.manage().window().resize_to(1280, 800)
  end

  after(:all) do
    driver.quit unless debugging?
  end

  before(:each) do
    driver.get("https://travel.agileway.net")
  end

  it "Regular User Sign in OK" do
    driver.find_element(:id, "username").send_keys("agileway")
    driver.find_element(:name, "password").send_keys("testwise")
    driver.find_element(:name, "commit").click
    expect(driver.find_element(:id, "flash_notice").text).to eq("Signed in!")
  end

  it "Admin User sign in OK" do
    driver.find_element(:id, "username").send_keys("admin")
    driver.find_element(:name, "password").send_keys("secret")
    driver.find_element(:name, "commit").click
    expect(driver.find_element(:id, "flash_notice").text).to eq("Signed in!")
  end
end
```

Playwright Test

Playwright Test provides a `test` function to declare tests and `expect` function for assertions. In contrast to Selenium with RSpec, Playwright Test is clearly more integrated.

The good news is that, aside from the language difference (JavaScript vs Ruby), Playwright Test closely resembles RSpec. Here's an example from the official Playwright documentation.

```
test.beforeEach(async ({ page }) => {
  console.log(`Running ${test.info().title}`);
  await page.goto('https://my.start.url/');
});

test('basic test', async ({ page }) => {
  await page.goto('https://playwright.dev/');
  const name = await page.innerText('.navbar__title');
  expect(name).toBe('Playwright');
});
```

Task 1. Navigate to a URL

```
await page.goto('https://...');
```

Task 2. Execute test script file (multiple test cases)

If you are using TestWise IDE, the instruction is the same as for executing RSpec (see the above).

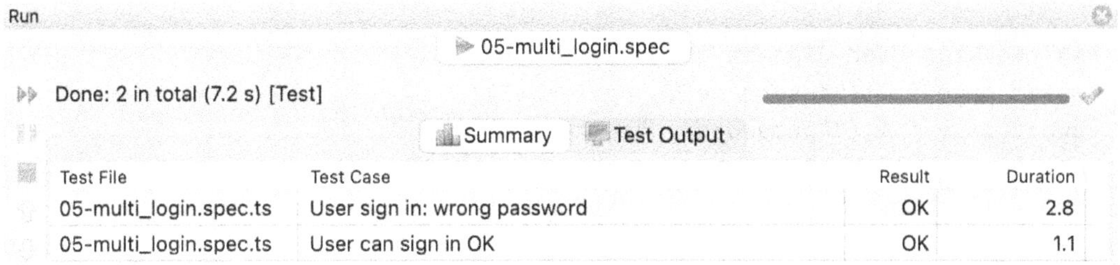

Figure 7. The output (in TestWise) of exeucting one single Playwright Test script, containing two test cases.

If you are using Visual Studio, see the instruction in Appendix.

Task 3. Optimize the test scripts to use `before(:each)` hook

```
test.beforeEach(async () => {
  await page.goto("https://...");
});
```

Full Test Script (Playwright Test)

```
import { test, Page, expect } from '@playwright/test';
var path = require("path");

test.describe.configure({ mode: 'serial' });

import * as Helper from '../test_helper.js'

test.beforeAll(async ({ browser }) => {
  page = await browser.newPage();
});

test.afterAll(async () => {
   await page.close();
});

test.beforeEach(async () => {
  await page.goto("https://travel.agileway.net");
});

test('Regular User Sign in OK', async () => {
  await page.fill("#username", "agileway");
  await page.fill("#password", "testwise");
  await page.click("input:has-text('Sign in')");
  const flashText = await page.textContent("#flash_notice")
  expect(flashText).toEqual('Signed in!');
});

test('Admin User can sign in OK', async () => {
  await page.fill("#username", "admin");
  await page.fill("#password", "secret");
  await page.click("input:has-text('Sign in')");
  const flashText = await page.textContent("#flash_notice")
```

```
    expect(flashText).toEqual('Signed in!');
});
```

6: Alternative Login Tests

Up to this point, the two automated user login tests follow Happy Path[1], testing default scenario featuring no exceptional or error conditions. Of course, there are "Unhappy Paths" (a formal name is 'Alternative Paths'; Zhimin sometimes refer as 'Sad Paths'), such as a test scenario where a user is unable to log in with an incorrect password.

Exercise 06

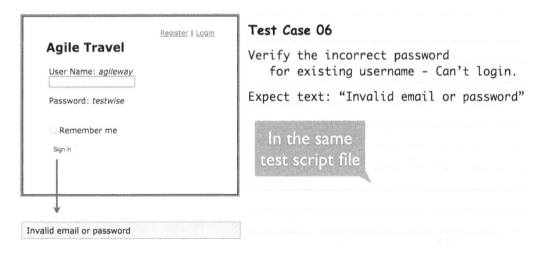

This is essentially a variation of Ex04 (a happy path user login test), but with two additional login failure test cases included in the same test script. Special note: Place the two alternative tests before the happy-path test case *(there is a good reason for this special requirement, to be revealed in the next exercise)*.

When scripting, it's generally discouraged to copy and paste. Writing the scripts manually is often more efficient and helps maintain a streamlined workflow. We will also show some productivity tips to further improve your scripting process.

---

[1]https://en.wikipedia.org/wiki/Happy_path

Learning Objectives

- Review

    - Selenium `find_element` syntax with ID locator
    - RSpec test structure
    - Playwright Test structure

- TestWise Productivity Tips:

    - Validation
    - TestWise Snippet
    - Reformat (pretty-printing)
    - Code Completion (sort of)
    - Script Library

Test Design

- Starting with Ex04 test script.
- Add one "User failed to sign in: the user name not exists" as the first test case.
- Add one "User failed to sign in: the password is invalid" as the second test case.

Test data preparation

The exercise instructions do not specify test data, such as which incorrect password to use. One of the responsibilities of Test Automation Engineers is to create the test data required for automated scripts. For this exercise, the test data preparation is fairly simple. In future exercises, we will explore techniques for handling more complex scenarios.

TestWise Productivity Tips (Selenium)

We utilize tools to enhance productivity, which is essential for effective end-to-end (E2E) test automation. If you're not using TestWise IDE, look for similar features in the testing tool you prefer.

Tip 1. Faster (and Safer) Typing Selenium Statements

The first challenge for new-to-Selenium-automation testers is typing Selenium statements correctly. When that happens (very common), the attendees are frustrated.

As a coach, Zhimin worked out a simple approach to overcome the following issues bothering beginners.

- Not remembering the Selenium syntax
- Slow typing
- Typos

Selenium syntax is quite simple (as below), still, beginners will take some time to get used to it.

```
driver.find_element(:id, "login-btn").click
driver.find_element(:name, "username").send_keys("ABC")
```

A simple solution to use Snippets in TestWise. Watch the video below.

Video 2: TestWise Snippets[2]

To help you remember: `d` is shorthand for `driver`, `fe` for `find_element`.

`dfe` → `driver.find_element(:how, "what")`, → means typing a **Tab** key to expand. This is a generic selenium statement, users need to replace `:how` and "what".

Normally, we append another character for a specific locator.

---

[2]https://youtu.be/sh-BsCHCTno

```
dfei → driver.find_element(:id, "id")
dfel → driver.find_element(:link_text, "Link")
dfen → driver.find_element(:name, "Name")
```

You get the idea.

Tip 2. Script Validation

Automated test scripts need to conform to a certain format, in this case, RSpec (and Ruby). In other words, to run a RSpec test script, it must be a valid Ruby script first.

A common reason that a beginner's test script does not run: the test script is an invalid script syntax (Ruby or JavaScript).

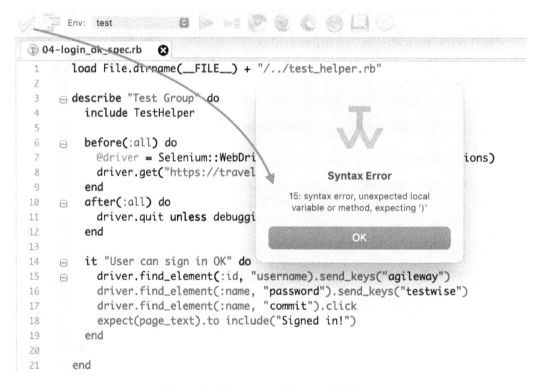

Figure 8. A test script fails on validation.

The error is "*15: syntax error, unexpected local variable or method, expecting ')'*". This indicated the possible error on line 15. Thanks to the syntax highlighting (in TestWise), it is quite easy to spot a missing right double quote after username.

Please note, the error line number in the validation message is only indicative.

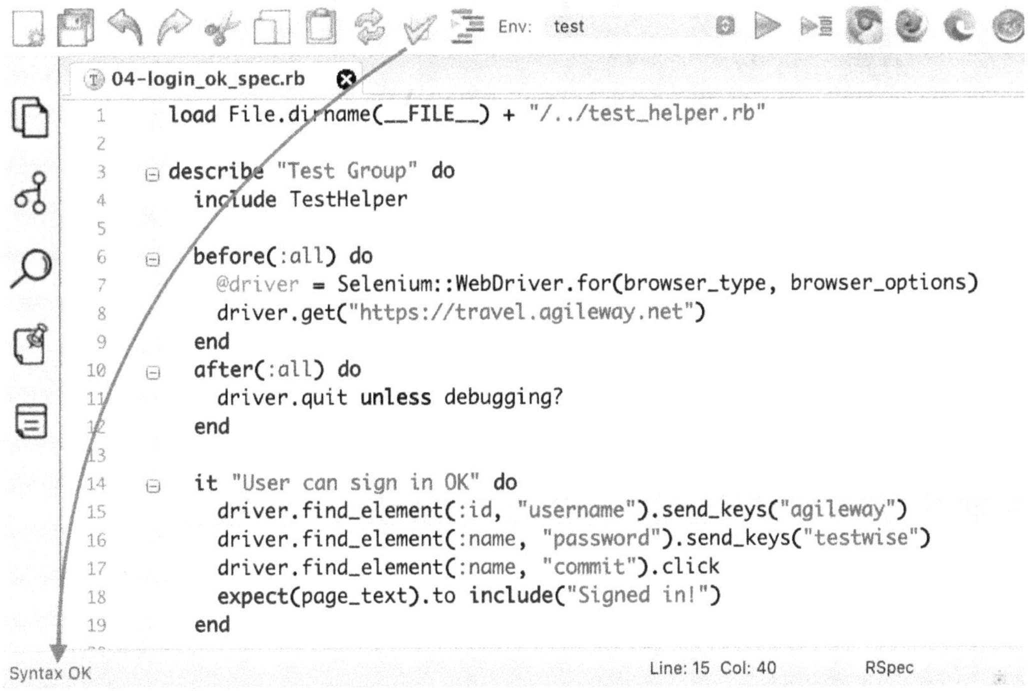

Figure 9. Test script passes validation.

Tip 3. Reformat

New-to-coding testers' first test scripts often end up like the below.

```
ⓘ 04-login_ok_spec.rb *    ✕

 3    ⊟ describe "Test Group" do
 4          include TestHelper
 5
 6    ⊟      before(:all) do
 7            @driver = Selenium::WebDriver.for(browser_type, browser_options)
 8               driver.get("https://travel.agileway.net")
 9          end
10    ⊟ after(:all) do
11                      driver.quit unless debugging?
12          end
13
14    ⊟      it "User can sign in OK" do
15               driver.find_element(:id, "username").send_keys("agileway")
16
17            driver.find_element(:name, "password").send_keys("testwise")
18          driver.find_element(:name, "commit").click
19               expect(page_text).to include("Signed in!")
20        end
21        end
```

Click the 'reformat' button (as indicated below) on the toolbar to reformat the test
script.

```
1    load File.dirname(__FILE__) + "/../test_helper.rb"
2
3  ⊟ describe "Test Group" do
4      include TestHelper
5
6  ⊟    before(:all) do
7        @driver = Selenium::WebDriver.for(browser_type, browser_options)
8        driver.get("https://travel.agileway.net")
9      end
10 ⊟    after(:all) do
11       driver.quit unless debugging?
12     end
13
14 ⊟    it "User can sign in OK" do
15       driver.find_element(:id, "username").send_keys("agileway")
16
17       driver.find_element(:name, "password").send_keys("testwise")
18       driver.find_element(:name, "commit").click
19       expect(page_text).to include("Signed in!")
20     end
21   end
```

Figure 10. Reformat a test script file

This looks much better (it is called proper indenting), right? That's why "code reformat" is also known as "pretty printing". Not only that, this will it much easier to spot syntax errors.

Tip 4. IntelliSense (sort of)

IntelliSense is a code-completion aid. Ruby is a dynamic language and TestWise a not a coding IDE, so the code-completion support is limited in TestWise. Still, it is quite useful.

Let us illustrate with an example, please try it yourself as well. After dfen and followed by a Tab key, type ".".

```
driver.find_element(:id, "username").
```
```
  text
  click
  submit
```

TestWise will populate available Selenium operations to choose from. Type characters ("se" in the example below) to narrow down the options list.

```
driver.find_element(:id, "username").sel
```
```
  send_keys(key_sequences)
  selected?
```

Press the "**Enter**" key to select.

Tip 5. Script Library

Beginners can complete this exercise under coaching. When practising this or similar test script alone, they often run into problems: they forget some syntax.

There is a way, to use the "Script Library" (not test best name, we know) in TestWise.

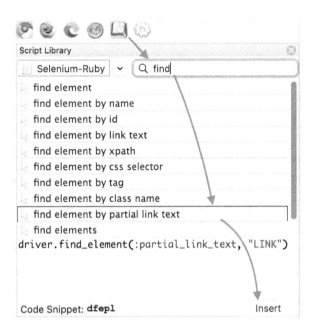

Click the "**Insert**" button to add the selected selenium statement into the editor (test script).

Visual Studio Code (Playwright)

1. Snippet Statements

Snippets are pre-written code segments that are especially useful for beginners. They provide shortcuts to help you work faster and minimize errors.

The basic Playwright VS Code extension does not include snippet support. However, other VS Code extensions can add this functionality. Among the available options, the most popular one is Nitay Neeman's Playwright Snippets[3].

Then, when writing a Playwright test, use the pw keyword to trigger a popup of possible snippets (type more to narrow down the search and use **Enter** to select).

---

[3]https://marketplace.visualstudio.com/items?itemName=nitayneeman.playwright-snippets

```
test('User can sign in OK', async () => {
    pw-f
});   ┌─────────────────────────────────────────────────────┐
      │ ☐ pw-page-fill                          page.fill   │
      └─────────────────────────────────────────────────────┘
        ☐ pw-page-focus                          page.focus
        ☐ pw-import-firefox                  Import Firefox
```

In the example above, selecting the `fill` suggestion and pressing Enter will automatically replace the line with a default `await page.fill('', '');` statement.

```
test('User can sign in OK', async () => {
    await page.fill('|', '');
});
```

This is really helpful and I can recommend using Snippets. However, one thing to note is that this extension expands snippets to the `page.<action>` format, instead of Playwright's officially recommended syntax `page.locator().<action>`.

2. IntelliSense Auto-Completion

The auto-code completion from the basic Visual Studio Code Playwright plugin is quite good. As you type, it suggests available methods, narrowing down the options as you enter more characters. For instance, typing `f` will display suggestions like fill, frame, and others.

```
test('User can sign in OK', async () => {
    await page.locator("#username").f;
});              ⊕ fill          (method) Locator.fill(value: string, opti...
                ⊕ filter
                ⊕ first
                ⊕ focus
                ⊕ frameLocator
```

Press the **Enter** key to select the suggestion.

Test Script

For conciseness, we will only show test cases and it's related parts; and omit the surrounding sections.

Selenium RSpec

```
before(:each) do
  driver.get("https://travel.agileway.net")
end

it "User sign in but username not exists" do
  driver.find_element(:id, "username").send_keys("baduser")
  driver.find_element(:name, "password").send_keys("testwise")
  driver.find_element(:name, "commit").click
  expect(page_text).to include("Invalid email or password")
end

it "User sign in with wrong password" do
  driver.find_element(:id, "username").send_keys("agileway")
  driver.find_element(:name, "password").send_keys("baspass")
  driver.find_element(:name, "commit").click
  expect(driver.find_element(:id, "flash_alert").text).to
    include("Invalid email or password")
end

it "User can sign in OK" do
  driver.find_element(:id, "username").send_keys("agileway")
  driver.find_element(:name, "password").send_keys("testwise")
  driver.find_element(:name, "commit").click
  expect(page_text).to include("Signed in!")
end
```

Playwright Test

```javascript
test.beforeEach(async () => {
  await page.goto(Helper.site_url());
});

test('User sign in but username not exists', async () => {
  await page.fill("#username", "baduser");
  await page.fill("#password", "testwise");
  await page.click("input:has-text('Sign in')");
  const flashText = await page.textContent("#flash_alert")
  expect(flashText).toEqual('Invalid email or password');
});

test('User sign in with wrong password', async () => {
  await page.fill("#username", "agileway");
  await page.fill("#password", "badpass");
  await page.click("input:has-text('Sign in')");
  const flashText = await page.textContent("#flash_alert")
  expect(flashText).toEqual('Invalid email or password');
});

test('User can sign in OK', async () => {
  await page.fill("#username", "agileway");
  await page.fill("#password", "testwise");
  await page.click("input:has-text('Sign in')");
  const flashText = await page.textContent("#flash_notice")
  expect(flashText).toEqual('Signed in!');
});
```

7: Test Execution Side Effects

In previous exercises (Ex04, Ex05, and Ex06), we focused on user login testing, incorporating key test automation concepts and techniques. In this exercise, we will continue testing user login functionality but with a real-world testing approach.

What does this mean? Typically, when designing automated tests for a requirement, we start with the "happy path"—in this case, a successful "sign-in OK" scenario. Afterward, we may add one or more alternative paths. You might recall that in Ex06, we explicitly asked you to place two alternative-path test cases in the front of the 'happy-path' one. You will understand why after completing this exercise.

We also recommend starting from scratch with a new test project and applying what you've learned in the previous exercises.

Exercise 07

The test scenario remains the same: testing user sign-in on the AgileTravel site, but with a different focus.

Task 07

```
Run individual tests
   Positive test - Sign in OK
   Negative test - Sign in failed

Run both test cases (in the same script file)
   Make both tests pass
```

Test Data

```
Site URL:     https://travel.agileway.net
User Login:   'agileway' / 'testwise'
```

Learning Objectives

- Run test file vs Run test case
- Test Development Rhythm

  - Run test case
  - Run test script file (all test cases)

- Test Execution side effect
- Review: Snippets, Script Validation, Reformat, Code Library, ... ,etc
- Review: Comment out scripts (exclude from execution)

Tasks

Task Execution Rhythm

1. Run test case (one by one)
2. Until each execution of an individual test case pass
3. Run the test script (all test cases in it)

Task 1. Run two test cases individually, one by one

Right-click any line between the test case "User can sign in OK", and run this test case (first option, as indicated below).

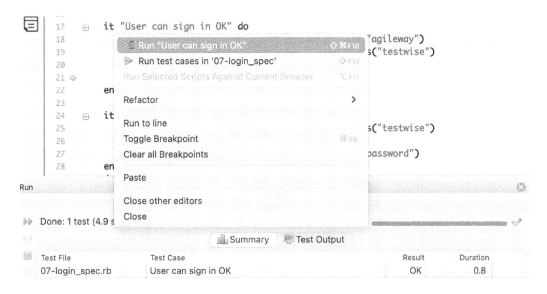

The test execution was successful. Now run the second test case "User can sign in failed".

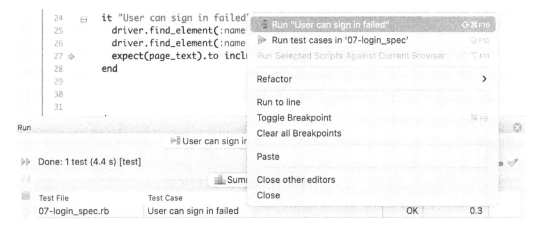

This test execution was successful too.

Task 2. Run the test script (i.e. all test cases)

A test script file, such as xxx_spec.rb, may contain one or more test cases. In TestWise, click the blue play button (as shown below) to run the test script, which will execute all the test cases in the file.

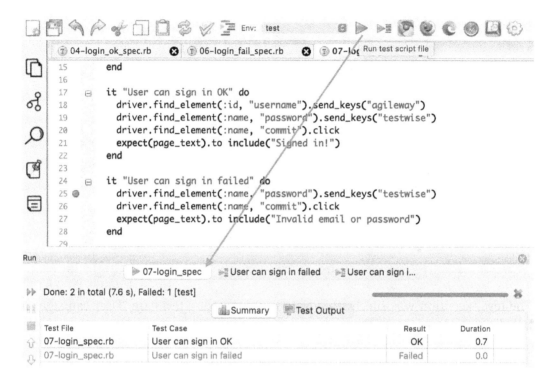

Can you guess the results? Just a reminder, both test cases (within the same script file) passed.

The second test case failed! There were no changes to the script. If you reran the second test, it would pass as well. The only logical explanation is something to do with the execution of the first test case.

Knowledge Point: Execution Side Effect

We can treat the target application in one browser window as a shared resource; any test execution (manual or automated) can change its state, affecting the upcoming test executions. This is an important concept in Software Testing. It is a common concept but is made obvious in test automation.

In this exercise, the execution of the first test case affected the second. Let's follow the state of the application in the browser window.

- Browser launched by Selenium (*sign-in state: No*)

- After execution of the first test case (*sign-in state: Yes*)
- Before the execution of the second test case (*sign-in state: Yes*)
- Trying to sign in again failed! Why? Already signed in.

Knowledge Point: Two Test Execution Modes

Before we explain the differences between the two execution modes (test case and test script), have a look at this 'after(:all)' block (in all of our test scripts).

```
after(:all) do
  driver.quit unless debugging?
end
```

1. **Execute a single test case**

   The debugging? flag is set to true (via TestWise). Therefore, the browser will be left open.

2. **Execute a test script file**

   i.e., all the test cases in this test script file. The debugging? flag is set to false (via TestWise). The browser window will close after test execution in this mode.

Task 3. Analyse and Fix

After the execution of the first test case, the user is logged in successfully in the browser. The second test tried to continue from there, expecting the login page. That's why it failed on the first line (line 29) of the second test case.

To fix this, we want a clean state, i.e., not logged-in state, before each test case.

Approach 1: Swap the order of two test cases (not recommended)

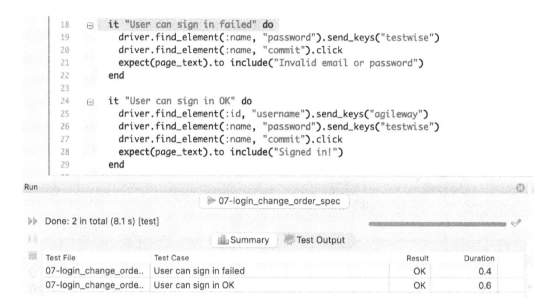

```
18  ⊟   it "User can sign in failed" do
19          driver.find_element(:name, "password").send_keys("testwise")
20          driver.find_element(:name, "commit").click
21          expect(page_text).to include("Invalid email or password")
22      end
23
24  ⊟   it "User can sign in OK" do
25          driver.find_element(:id, "username").send_keys("agileway")
26          driver.find_element(:name, "password").send_keys("testwise")
27          driver.find_element(:name, "commit").click
28          expect(page_text).to include("Signed in!")
29      end
```

Run   ⊗

                          ▶ 07-login_change_order_spec

▷▷ Done: 2 in total (8.1 s) [test]   ━━━━━━━━━━━━ ✓

                          📊 Summary   🖥 Test Output

Test File	Test Case	Result	Duration
07-login_change_orde..	User can sign in failed	OK	0.4
07-login_change_orde..	User can sign in OK	OK	0.6

This is acceptable but not optimal. Ideally, we want each test case independent of others, including the execution order.

Approach 2: Clear the side effects

A more intuitive approach is to sign out at the end of the successful login test case. You've likely done this during manual testing without even noticing. In test automation, however, we need to explicitly include this step.

To achieve this, add a sign-out step to the end of the first "Sign in OK" test case:

```
driver.find_element(:link_text, "Sign off (agileway)").click
```

Run the whole test script, pass!

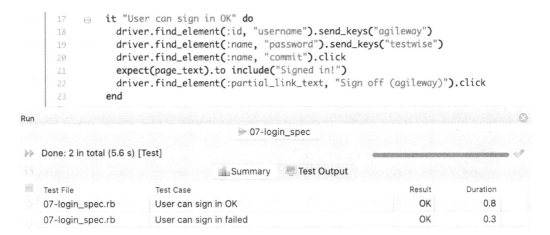

```
17    it "User can sign in OK" do
18      driver.find_element(:id, "username").send_keys("agileway")
19      driver.find_element(:name, "password").send_keys("testwise")
20      driver.find_element(:name, "commit").click
21      expect(page_text).to include("Signed in!")
22      driver.find_element(:partial_link_text, "Sign off (agileway)").click
23    end
```

Test File	Test Case	Result	Duration
07-login_spec.rb	User can sign in OK	OK	0.8
07-login_spec.rb	User can sign in failed	OK	0.3

Figure 11. Click "Sign off" to log out after the sign in Ok test

Task 4. Make the sign off step works for any user

In Ex05, we have test cases for signing in as different users, such as 'admin' and 'agileway'. As you may have noticed, the sign-off link text is now dynamic (since December 2024), displaying the usernames, e.g., 'Sign off (admin)' and 'Sign off (agileway)'. Can you use a single Selenium test step for signing off, regardless of who is signed in?

This is a perfect case to use another Selenium locator: "PARTIAL_LINK_TEXT".

```
driver.find_element(:partial_link_text, "Sign off").click
```

Playwright

1. **Click a link with partial text**

```
await page.locator('text=Sign off').click();
```

Pay attention to the locator string.

- `text=Sign off`
  Case-insensitive and searches for a substring.

- `text="Sign off"`
  Search for a text node with exact string.

 We think the Selenium WebDriver syntax is clearly superior in this case.

Test Scripts

Selenium WebDriver + RSpec

```
before(:all) do
  @driver = Selenium::WebDriver.for(browser_type, browser_options)
  driver.get("https://travel.agileway.net")
end

it "User can sign in OK" do
  driver.find_element(:id, "username").send_keys("agileway")
  driver.find_element(:name, "password").send_keys("testwise")
  driver.find_element(:name, "commit").click
  expect(page_text).to include("Signed in!")
  driver.find_element(:partial_link_text, "Sign off").click
end

it "User can sign in failed" do
  driver.find_element(:name, "password").send_keys("testwise")
  driver.find_element(:name, "commit").click
  expect(page_text).to include("Invalid email or password")
end
```

Playwright Test

```
test.beforeEach(async () => {
  await page.goto("https://travel.agileway.net");
});

test('User can sign in OK', async () => {
  await page.fill("#username", "agileway");
  await page.fill("#password", "testwise");
  await page.click("input:has-text('Sign in')");
  const flashText = await page.textContent("#flash_notice")
  expect(flashText).toEqual('Signed in!');
  page.locator('text=Sign off').click();
});

test('User sign in with wrong password', async () => {
  await page.fill("#username", "agileway");
  await page.fill("#password", "badpass");
  await page.click("input:has-text('Sign in')");
  const flashText = await page.textContent("#flash_alert")
  expect(flashText).toEqual('Invalid email or password');
});
```

FAQ

1. **If I put just one test case in one test script file, will that solve the dependency problem?**

   No, one test case per test script prevents dependencies between test cases. But there can also be dependencies between test scripts. We will cover that topic in later chapters.

2. **Why do you put more than one test case in one test script file?**

   Grouping related test cases in one test script will help you manage them better and execute them faster. Furthermore, it provides opportunities for script reuse. Again, we will cover that in later chapters.

8: Select One-way Flight

We move on, from user login, to the business scenarios of Agile Travel site.

Exercise 08

After login (Ex04), perform the four steps as shown in the task card. Ignore the selecting departing dates for now.

 Tip: Perform manual testing first.

Learning Objectives

• Reusing scripts

- Clone an existing test script file
- XPath Locators
- Drive a Select (Combo) box in Selenium WebDriver & Playwright
- Review

  – TestWise debugging mode
  – Working on individual test steps (one by one) in TestWise debugging mode
  – Copy the working test steps over to complete the test script.

Focused Test Design

A simple yet effective test design approach is to focus each test scenario on a specific web page. For example, the two user login tests we did for the login page in the previous exercise. After the user successfully signs in to Agile Travel, the next page is the "Select Flight" page. In this exercise, we will develop one test case for the "One-way flight," and in the next exercise, we'll create a test case for the "Return flight."

By the way, Zhimin worked out this approach in 2007 and named it "Focused Test Design".

Test Design

This will be a new test script file.

- Start a new test script
- Can copy over the previous login steps over.
- Click the one-way radio button
- Select a departure city
- Select a destination city
- Click the continue button
- Assert "the departure city to the destination city"

Tasks

Task 1. Clone an existing test script (TestWise)

We already have a working `login_spec.rb` and know that this "Select one-way flight" test script begins with the login steps. An effective approach is to clone the `login_spec.rb` and modify it to include the test steps relevant to the new test script.

Highlight the login script file (`04-login_spec.rb`) and select "**Refactor**" → "Copy File ...".

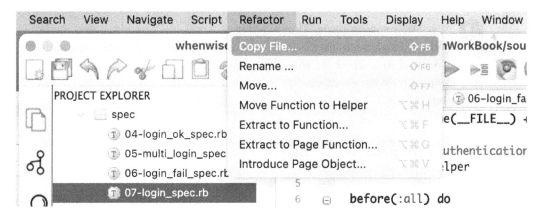

In the "Copy File" dialog, enter the new file name, in this case, `08-select_flight_-spec.rb`.

> You may change it to a different name if you wish. This is a RSpec test script file, so it must end with `_spec.rb`.
>
> Also, do not include spaces or special characters in a file name.

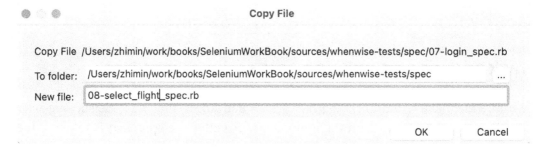

A new test script file `08-select_flight_spec.rb` will be created with the content from the `login_spec.rb`.

> Tip: After copy-n-paste, Zhimin habitually puts hisi mind into alert mode. Why? *"I have been 'lazy'"*. In end to end test automation, quite commonly, we need to alter or do something with copied test steps. In short, use copied code with caution. We'll discuss this further when introducing test refactoring.

Update the "test group name" and "test case name".

```ruby
describe "Select Flights" do
  include TestHelper

  before(:all) do
    @driver = Selenium::WebDriver.for(browser_type, browser_options)
    driver.manage().window().resize_to(1280, 800)
    driver.get("https://travel.agileway.net")
  end

  after(:all) do
    driver.quit unless debugging?
  end

  it "User can select one way trip" do
    driver.find_element(:id, "username").send_keys("agileway")
    driver.find_element(:name, "password").send_keys("testwise")
    driver.find_element(:name, "commit").click
    expect(page_text).to include("Signed in!")
```

```
    # ...
  end

end
```

Also, append # ... (*comment*) to remind that the test case is incomplete.

Task 2. Start developing a new test case, one-way trip.

Repeat the process of how we did our login test:

1. **Run the test case** (*individual test execution mode*)

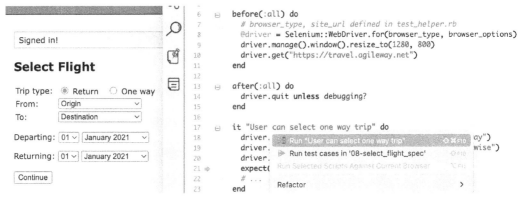

2. **After the test execution completes, focus on the Chrome browser window.**
3. **Prepare to inspect the control of the next operation**, in this case, the "one-way radio button". (*you did manual testing first, right?*)

Task 3. Click the one-way radio button

Right-click the radio button, and get its HTML:

```
<input type="radio" name="tripType" value="oneway"
       onclick="$('#returnTrip').hide();">
```

There is no ID, seems a good case for the NAME locator.

Select one test step to get into TestWise Debugging mode.

```
17   ⊟   it "User can select one way trip" do
18          driver.find_element(:id, "username").send_keys("agileway")
19          driver.find_element(:name, "password").send_keys("testwise")
20          driver.find_element(:name, "commit").click
21 ⇨        expect(page_text).to include("Signed in!")
22          # ...                                ▶≣ Run "User can select one way trip"    ⇧ ⌘F10
23      end                                       ▷ Run test cases in '08-select_flight_spec'  ⇧F10
24                                                Run Selected Scripts Against Current Browser   ⌥F11
```

In the special debugging test case, type the statement to click the one-way radio button (using snippet: dfen).

```
13   ⊟   it "Debugging" do
14 ⇨        driver.find_element(:name, "tripType").click
15
16      end
```

Run this special debugging test case, but no effect. Manually select the one-way radio button, and run the debugging test again. Something changed: the "Return" radio button is selected. Why?

Inspect the "Return" radio button, you will find that these two buttons are together (in HTML).

```
<td>
  <input type="radio" name="tripType" checked="true"
    onclick="$('#returnTrip').show();" value="return"> Return  
  <input type="radio" name="tripType" value="oneway"
    onclick="$('#returnTrip').hide();"> One way
</td>
```

Both buttons share the same NAME! So, we cannot use the name attribute, probably the VALUE attribute, but there is no such locator in Selenium.

Knowledge point: XPath Locator

So far, you have used three (out of eight) locators: **ID**, **NAME**, and **LINK**. Now, the fourth: **XPath**, the most powerful one. It might sound complex (which can be),

Zhimin came up with a simple Xpath syntax that shall work >90% of cases *(based on his usage stats)*.

First of all, the snippet (as you guessed): `dfex` → `driver.find_element(:xpath, "…")`.

```
<p>
  <input type="submit" name="commit" value="Sign in"
  data-disable-with="Sign in"> == $0
</p>
```

Zhimin's Simple Way of Using XPath

"`//tag_name[@attr='…']`"

```
driver.find_element(:xpath,"//input[@value='Sign in']")
```

Let's try it out for the one-way radio button.

- tag_name: `input`
- attribute name: `value`
- attribute value: `oneway`

The resulting statement is

```
driver.find_element(:xpath, "//input[@value='oneway']").click
```

Beginners usually make the following four typos:

- Just one leading slash /, it should be two.
- Mismatched square brackets [ ].
- Missing @ in the front of the attribute name.
- Did not wrap the string value with two single quotes.

– You can use single quotes for the outer part of the XPath expression and
double quotes for the string values inside. This is a personal preference,
but the key point is that the quotes must be different unless you escape
them. For beginners, avoid escaping for now and stick to this simple syntax
pattern.*

Yes, possibly four typing errors for just 24 characters. Our advice to beginners: don't
be eager to type it in TestWise yet. Read the above and try to understand (or just
memorize for 30 seconds).

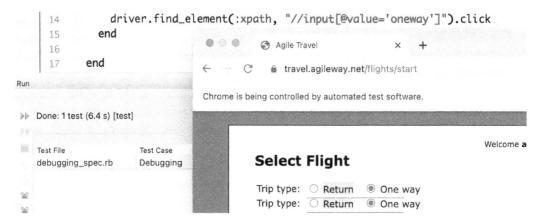

Anyway, if typed correctly, the above statement works (try it in debugging mode).

Task 4. Select a city from a drop-down list.

The following two operations are the same type of operation: select an option in a
dropdown list. The formal name for this kind of control is Select List.

Right-click inspect the from city select list, and get its HTML:

```
<select name="fromPort" style="width:150px;">
   <option value="">Origin</option>
   <option>New York</option>
   <option value="sydney">Sydney</option>
   <option>San Francisco</option>
</select>
```

Knowledge point: Select an option in a Select List.

A Select List a combo control in HTML. You have seen Links and Buttons, both of which only have one tag (in HTML). A Select List has two tags.

- One select
- One or many options

1. Inspect as usual

```
▼<lu>
  ▼<select name="fromPort" style="width:150px;"> == $0
     <option value=Origin</option>  slot
     <option>New York</option>  slot
     <option>Sydney</option>  slot
     <option>San Francisco</option>  slot
  </select>
```

2. Drive it: two steps   Has two tags!

```
Selenium::WebDriver::Support::Select.new(driver.find_eleme
nt(:name, "fromPort")).select_by(:text, "Sydney")
```

We am going to show the selenium statement to select "Sydney" in the from city dropdown.

```
Selenium::WebDriver::Support::Select.new(
  driver.find_element(:name, "fromPort")).select_by(:text, "Sydney")
```

It is quite complex, isn't it? Don't worry, Zhimin has written thousands of driving dropdown statements, but he still sometimes doesn't remember the above. How? using a snippet.

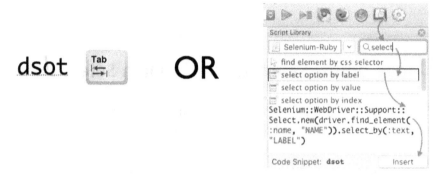

Type dsot (means, drive select option by text), followed by a Tab key. You get

```
Selenium::WebDriver::Support::Select.new(driver.find_element(:name, "select_name")).select_by(:text, "text")
```

Then type the NAME (in this case, 'fromPort',) another Tab key, and type the option text (in this case, 'Sydney').

It is actually easier than it sounds.

In addition to selecting an option by label, we can also select it by value or index.

```
elem = driver.find_element(:name, "fromPort")
Selenium::WebDriver::Support::Select.new(elem).select_by(:index, 1)
Selenium::WebDriver::Support::Select.new(elem).select_by(:value, "sydney")
```

Task 5. Complete the remaining test steps in debugging mode.

After selecting the departure and destination city, there are still two operations:

1. **Click the 'Continue' button,**

Another use of the XPath locator.

2. **Assert the text "Sydney to New York" on the next page**.

Standard "page text include" check.

```
it "Debugging" do
  #driver.find_element(:xpath, "//input[@value='oneway']").click
  #Selenium::WebDriver::Support::Select.new(driver.find_element(:name, "fromPort")).select_by(:text, "Sydney")
  #Selenium::WebDriver::Support::Select.new(driver.find_element(:name, "toPort")).select_by(:text, "New York")
  #driver.find_element(:xpath, "//input[@value='Continue']").click
  expect(page_text).to include("Sydney to New York")
end
```

Copy the steps to the main test script (and uncommented steps). Run the test case.

Playwright Test

1. **XPath Locator**

Playwright also supports XPath locators, although they are not as clearly defined as in Selenium WebDriver. The syntax is:

```
await page.locator("xpath=//input[@value='oneway']").click();
```

Always handcraft XPath locators

Playwright documentation suggests[1], "*If you absolutely must use CSS or XPath locators...*", implying that using XPath locators is generally discouraged. The reasoning is that "*CSS and XPath are not recommended as the DOM can often change, leading to non-resilient tests.*"

We disagree. The issue often lies with poor XPath expressions, such as '//*[@id="tsf"]/div[2]/div[1]/div[1]/div/div[2]/input'. These kind of low-quality locators are typically created by inexperienced testers relying on recording tools or using Chrome's "Copy Full XPath" functionality.

When working with elements that lack clear and simple identifiers like ID

> or NAME, a well-crafted XPath is often the best solution. XPath locator has a unique and powerful feature: bidirectionality, meaning they can locate elements both from top to bottom and bottom to top. We will demonstrate this in later exercises.

- **Select an option in a dropdown list**

```
await page.locator("select[name='toPort']").selectOption({label: 'Sydney'})
```

An alternative syntax, less preferred by Playwright, is:

```
await page.selectOption("select[name='toPort']", { label: 'New York' });
```

In addition to selecting an option by label, we can also select it by value or index.

```
await page.locator("#departDay").selectOption({ index: 2 });
await page.locator("#departMonth").selectOption("032025");
```

Test Script

Selenium + RSpec

---

[1]https://playwright.dev/docs/locators

```ruby
it "User can select one way trip" do
  driver.get("https://travel.agileway.net")
  driver.find_element(:id, "username").send_keys("agileway")
  driver.find_element(:name, "password").send_keys("testwise")
  driver.find_element(:name, "commit").click
  expect(page_text).to include("Signed in!")
  driver.find_element(:xpath, "//input[@value='oneway']").click
  Selenium::WebDriver::Support::Select.new(
    driver.find_element(:name, "fromPort")).select_by(:text, "Sydney")
  Selenium::WebDriver::Support::Select.new(
    driver.find_element(:name, "toPort")).select_by(:text, "New York")
  driver.find_element(:xpath, "//input[@value='Continue']").click
  expect(page_text).to include("Sydney to New York")
end
```

Playright Test

```javascript
test('User can select one way trip', async () => {
  await page.fill("#username", "agileway");
  await page.fill("#password", "testwise");
  await page.click("input:has-text('Sign in')");

  await page.locator("//input[@value='oneway']").click();
  await page.locator("select[name='fromPort']").selectOption(
    { label: 'Sydney' });
  await page.selectOption("select[name='toPort']", { label: 'New York' });
  await page.click("//input[@value='Continue']");
  const pageText = await page.textContent("body");
  expect(pageText).toContain("Sydney to New York");
});
```

9: Select Return Flight

After done "one-way flight" test case, naturally the next test case to write is "return flight", which is quite similar with just a couple of new steps.

Exercise 09

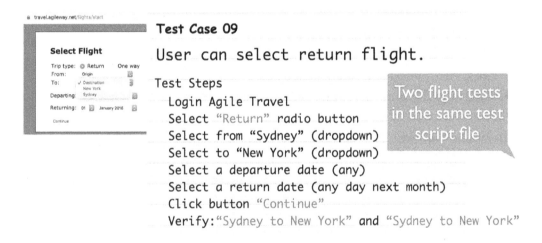

After implementing Ex09, ensure both tests (oneway and return) pass in this test script file.

Learning Objectives

- Review

  - XPath locators
  - Select an option in a dropdown list
  - Multiple test cases in one test script file

    – Two test execution modes (test script vs test case)
    – Test execution side-effect
    – Commenting

- Move shared steps to a `before(…)` execution hook.
- Debugging tip: keep the browser open temporarily in test script execution mode.

Test Design

- Login.
- Select "Return" flight (radio button).
- Choose a departure date (*day and month-year*) from a dropdown list.
- Choose a return date (*day and month-year*).
- Click the Continue button.
- Assert the flight information (including the dates) on the next page.

Readers who successfully completed the previous exercise may find this one relatively simple. While completing this test case alone is not challenging, ensuring that both the "one-way" and "return" tests pass is more difficult than it might initially thought.

Tasks

Task 1. Add the "selecting departure date" in "one-way flight" test.

This is a remaining task from the previous exercise—please complete it. Technically, use the same approach as selecting the "from-city" dropdown list.

As always, after interacting with a data input field, consider any necessary assertions that may be required.

Task 2. Click the 'Return' radio button.

There are no new concepts here, just another instance of driving a radio button; refer to Ex08. Please be sure to add assertion for the new test case too.

Don't copy-n-paste previous scripts. Instead, type (*using snippets*) to familiarise yourself with Selenium or Playwright syntax.

Task 3. Select departure and return dates from dropdown lists.

No new concepts are introduced here. This task involves four test steps that are technically similar. We encourage readers to experiment with different approaches. For instance, use an ID locator for `departDay` and a NAME locator for `returnDay`.

Task 4. Make the two tests pass.

There are two select-flight (one-way and return) tests in the same test script. Each test runs fine on its own. But when running the test script, the second test fails (which is quite common).

```
16    it "User can select one way trip" do
17       driver.find_element(:id, "username").send_keys("agileway")
18       driver.find_element(:name, "password").send_keys("testwise")
19       driver.find_element(:name, "commit").click
20       expect(page_text).to include("Signed in!")
21       driver.find_element(:xpath, "//input[@value='oneway']").click
22       Selenium::WebDriver::Support::Select.new(driver.find_element(:name, "fromPort")).select_by(:text, "Sydney")
23       Selenium::WebDriver::Support::Select.new(driver.find_element(:name, "toPort")).select_by(:text, "New York")
24       driver.find_element(:xpath, "//input[@value='Continue']").click
25       expect(page_text).to include("Sydney to New York")
26    end
27
28    it "User can select return  trip" do
29       driver.find_element(:id, "username").send_keys("agileway")
30       driver.find_element(:name, "password").send_keys("testwise")
31       driver.find_element(:name, "commit").click
32       expect(page_text).to include("Signed in!")
```

The cause is, of course, the execution side effect. But wait, if your test script is like the above, it has a design flaw: each test case has user sign-in steps.

When you manually test it, usually, you don't do sign-out and then sign-in for the second test. One logged-in user can perform two bookings within one user session.

From a testing perspective (focusing on flight selection), it is faster to perform within one user session.

Move the user login statements (in two test cases) into before(:all) block.

A question to consider: "Why not into the before(:each) *block?"*

```
 6  ⊟    before(:all) do
 7           @driver = Selenium::WebDriver.for(browser_type, browser_options)
 8           driver.manage().window().resize_to(1280, 800)
 9           driver.get("https://travel.agileway.net")
10           driver.find_element(:id, "username").send_keys("agileway")
11           driver.find_element(:name, "password").send_keys("testwise")
12           driver.find_element(:name, "commit").click
13           expect(page_text).to include("Signed in!")
14         end
15
16  ⊟    after(:all) do
17           driver.quit unless debugging?
18         end
19
20  ⊟    it "User can select one way trip" do
21           driver.find_element(:xpath, "//input[@value='oneway']").click
```

Run the test script again. It still fails.

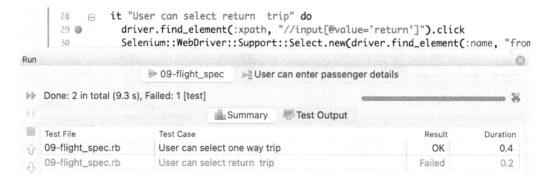

```
28  ⊟    it "User can select return  trip" do
29  ●        driver.find_element(:xpath, "//input[@value='return']").click
30           Selenium::WebDriver::Support::Select.new(driver.find_element(:name, "from
```

What happened here? The most logical approach is to inspect the browser window. However, the browser window is closed. When running individual test cases in TestWise, the browser window stays open. However, when executing the whole test script, it is standard practice to close the browser window to prevent multiple hanging browser windows when running the entire suite. So, how can we debug a scenario where all individual test executions pass, but the test script execution fails?

Debugging Tip: keep the browser open temporarily in "test script execution mode"

In test script execution mode (i.e., running the entire test script file), the browser window is closed by default. However, there are times when we may want to keep the browser open, such as for debugging or demonstration purposes.

Here is a simple workaround: comment out the `driver.quit` line.

```
after(:all) do
  # driver.quit unless debugging?
end
```

Run the test script again.

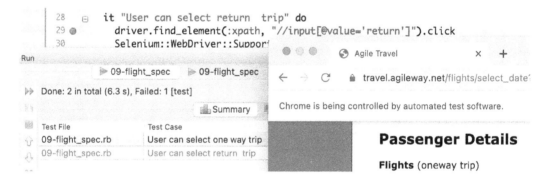

As we can see (in the browser window), after executing the first test case, we are on the passenger page, not the select flight page. No "return radio button" there.

After understanding the cause, the solution is easy. Navigate to the flight page: `https://travel.agileway.net/flights/start`.

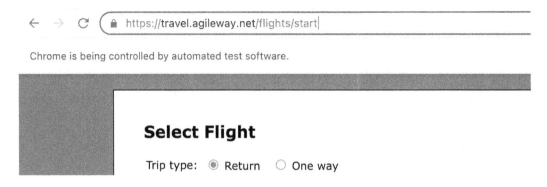

In Selenium: `driver.get("https://travel.agileway.net/flights/start")`. By the way, `driver.get()` is equivalant to `driver.navigate.to()`.

Run the test script again. Both tests pass!

```
28  ⊟   it "User can select return  trip" do
29          driver.get("https://travel.agileway.net/flights/start")
30          driver.find_element(:xpath, "//input[@value='return']").click
```

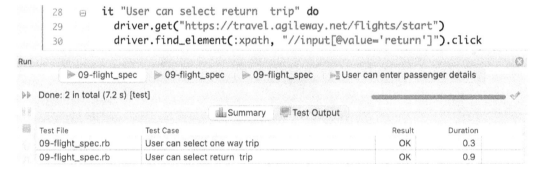

One more thing, don't forget to uncomment the close browser step in `after(:all)`.

```
after(:all) do
   driver.quit unless debugging?
end
```

Test Script

Selenium RSpec

```
load File.dirname(__FILE__) + "/../test_helper.rb"
describe "Select Flights" do
  include TestHelper

  before(:all) do
    @driver = Selenium::WebDriver.for(browser_type, browser_options)
    driver.get(site_url)
    driver.find_element(:id, "username").send_keys("agileway")
    driver.find_element(:name, "password").send_keys("testwise")
    driver.find_element(:name, "commit").click
  end

  after(:all) do
    driver.quit unless debugging?
  end

  it "User can select one way trip" do
    driver.find_element(:xpath, "//input[@value='oneway']").click
    Selenium::WebDriver::Support::Select.new(
      driver.find_element(:name, "fromPort")).select_by(:text, "Sydney")
    Selenium::WebDriver::Support::Select.new(
      driver.find_element(:name, "toPort")).select_by(:text, "New York")
    driver.find_element(:xpath, "//input[@value='Continue']").click
    expect(page_text).to include("Sydney to New York")
  end

  it "User can select return  trip" do
    driver.get("https://travel.agileway.net/flights/start")
    driver.find_element(:xpath, "//input[@value='return']").click
    Selenium::WebDriver::Support::Select.new(
      driver.find_element(:name, "fromPort")).select_by(:text, "Sydney")
    Selenium::WebDriver::Support::Select.new(
      driver.find_element(:name, "toPort")).select_by(:text, "New York")
    Selenium::WebDriver::Support::Select.new(
      driver.find_element(:id, "departDay")).select_by(:text, "02")
    Selenium::WebDriver::Support::Select.new(
      driver.find_element(:name, "departMonth")).select_by(:text, "March 2025")
    Selenium::WebDriver::Support::Select.new(
      driver.find_element(:xpath, "//select[@id='returnDay']")).select_by(:text\
, "03")
```

```
    Selenium::WebDriver::Support::Select.new(
      driver.find_element(:id, "returnMonth")).select_by(:text, "April 2025")
    driver.find_element(:xpath, "//input[@value='Continue']").click
    expect(page_text).to include("Sydney to New York")
    expect(page_text).to include("New York to Sydney")
  end
end
```

Playwright Test

```
import { test, Page, expect } from '@playwright/test';
test.describe.configure({ mode: 'serial' });
import * as Helper from '../test_helper.js'
let page: Page;

test.beforeAll(async ({ browser }) => {
  page = await browser.newPage();
  await page.goto(Helper.site_url());
  await page.fill("#username", "agileway");
  await page.fill("#password", "testwise");
  await page.click("input:has-text('Sign in')");
});

test.afterAll(async () => {
   await page.close();
});

test.beforeEach(async () => {
  await page.goto(Helper.site_url());
});

test('User can select one way trip', async () => {
  await page.locator("//input[@value='oneway']").click();
  await page.locator("select[name='fromPort']").selectOption({ label: 'Sydney' \
});
  await page.selectOption("select[name='toPort']", { label: 'New York' });
  await page.click("//input[@value='Continue']");
  const pageText = await page.textContent("body");
```

```
  expect(pageText).toContain("Sydney to New York");
});

test('User can select return trip', async () => {
  await page.locator("//input[@value='return']").click();
  await page.locator("select[name='fromPort']").selectOption({ label: 'Sydney' \
});
  await page.selectOption("select[name='toPort']", { label: 'New York' });
  await page.locator("#departDay").selectOption({ index: 2 });
  await page.locator("#departMonth").selectOption("032025");
  await page.locator("#returnDay").selectOption({ index: 3 });
  await page.locator("#returnMonth").selectOption("042025");
  await page.click("//input[@value='Continue']");
  const pageText = await page.textContent("body");
  expect(pageText).toContain("Sydney to New York");
  expect(pageText).toContain("New York to Sydney");
});
```

10: Enter Passenger Name

After selecting the flight in AgileTravel, the next page is to enter the passenger details.

Exercise 10

Passenger Details

Flights (oneway trip)

2021-01-01 **New York to Sydney**

Passenger details

First name: Bob
Last name: Tester
Next

travel.agileway.net/flights/passenger

Pay by Credit Card

Fare (*oneway New York to Sydney*): $959.00
Card type: ○ Visa   ○ Master
Card holder's name: Bob Tester

Test Case 10

User can enter passenger details

Login Agile Travel
Select flight (oneway or return)
Enter passenger name
Verify the name shown on the next page
      (As card holder's name)

Learning Objectives

- Review

    - Clone an existing test script
    - XPath locators

- Focused Test Design
- Assertions

    - page title
    - control's state
    - the text in a text box

- Introduce local variable (optional)

Test Design

The focus of this test case is on the passenger page: Login $\rightarrow$ Flight Page $\rightarrow$ Passenger Page. On the fight page, from the previous exercise, we have two options: one-way and return flights. Which one shall we choose in this test design?

- One-way flight, or
- Return flight, or
- Both

The correct answer is "One-way flight." Why? It is the quickest option to reach the Passenger page, the focus of this test scenario. Some readers who selected "Both" might argue, *"Doesn't this overlook the test scenario for a return flight with a passenger?"* That's a fair point. In theory, we should automate all possible test scenarios. However, in practice, there are limits to what can be done. As software testing engineers, we must assess and prioritize effectively.

> **Fact**: Few software teams have the capablity to maintain 50 end-to-end (via UI) automated tests, as regression testing.
>
> Zhimin has developed and maintained several large end-to-end test suites, each has 500+ Selenium RSpec tests, over the years. Does a 500-test suite cover every scenario? No! Far from it. Achieving 100% E2E test coverage is neither practical nor necessary. A valuable skill for a test automation engineer is the ability to determine which end-to-end tests should be included in the automation suite for regression testing. It's important to keep in mind that every end-to-end test incurs ongoing maintenance costs.

In an earlier chapter, we briefly introduced the concept of "Focused Test Design." Now, let's explore it through examples.

- In Login test script, focus on the user login scenarios:

  – Login OK
  – Login Failed

- In Flight test script, after "Login OK", focus on the flight scenarios:

  – One-way
  – Return

- In Passenger test script, after "Login OK" and "One-way", focus on just one scenario:

  – Enter the passenger names and verify on the next page

We don't worry about flight scenarios in the passenger test script, unless absolutely necessary. Because flight scenarios shall have been taken care of in the flight test script. In passenger test script, we focus on passenger-related scenarios. In test design, we choose the quickest (and simplest) way to navigate to the passenger page.

Knowledge Point: Assertion

A test case is incomplete without assertions. So far, we have been focused on driving controls using Selenium, with only one type of assertion: check page text contains "...". It is time to introduce a few more assertions in web testing.

Assert the page text contains

You have seen (and used) this assertion: verify a piece of text on the web page (visible).

```
expect(page_text).to include("Signed in!")
```

How does it work? There is no `driver.page_text` in Selenium. The `page_text` is a function in `test_helper.rb` (*created by TestWise*).

```
def page_text
  driver.find_element(:tag_name => "body").text
end
```

Here, we used another Selenium locator: **TAG_NAME**. Zhimin rarely uses this locator except for this use.

Let's quickly review the six (out of 8) Selenium locators that you have used.

- ID
- NAME
- LINK_TEXT
- XPATH
- PARTIAL_LINK_TEXT
- TAG_NAME

Zhimin uses the above six locators for 95+% Selenium steps. See, Selenium is quite easy, isn't it?

Assert the page title

```
driver.title
# example use
driver.get("testwisely.com")
expect(driver.title).to eq("TestWisely - Cloud based Continuous Testing lab")
```

eq means equals.

Assert a control's state

```
driver.find_element(:id, "sign_in_btn").enabled?
driver.find_element(:id, "special").displayed?
driver.find_element(:id, "remember_me").selected?

# example use
expect(driver.find_element(:id, "special").displayed?).to eq(true)
```

Please note the question mark in displayed?, which is one of many reasons we like Ruby scripting.

 Try the above out, in TestWise Debugging mode.

Assert a text control's value

We know how to 'type' text into a text box.

```
driver.find_element(:id, "username").send_keys("testwise")
```

To assert the text in a text box.

```
expect(driver.find_element(:id, "username")["value"]).to eq("testwise")
```

Tasks

Task 1. Create a new test script based on a flight test

- Clone the existing flight_spec.rb to a new test script file: passenger_spec.rb.
- Remove one flight test case, we suggest keeping the one-way one, because it is more concise (*faster*).
- Update test group and test case name
- Run the test case
- Enter TestWise debugging mode
- Start to work on the steps on the passenger name
- ...

Task 2. Verify the entered passenger name in a text box

```
expect(driver.find_element(:name, "holder_name")["value"]).to eq("Bob Tester")
```

Beginners might think the above is a bit long and get frustrated after getting typos.

To help you understand assertion better and avoid typos. Consider rewrite to the version below:

```
expected = "Bob Tester"
actual = driver.find_element(:name, "holder_name")["value"]
expect(actual).to eq(expected)
```

Do you think this version is better? If so, use it.

The `expected` and `actual` are called **variables** in programming. You can treat a variable x in Math, holding a value it is assigned (the right side of the = sign).

Using well-named variables make code (and scripts) more readble and sometimes more efficient.

Assertions in Playwright Test

1. **Page title**

```
const pageTitle = await page.title();
expect(pageTitle).toEqual("Agile Travel");
```

2. **Page text contains**

```
const pageText = await page.textContent("body");
expect(pageText).toContain("Welcome");
```

3. **A control's state**

```
await page.isEnabled("#sign_in_btn");
await page.locator("#sign_in_btn").isEnabled();

await page.isVisible("#special");
await page.locator("#special").isVisible();

await page.isChecked("#remember_me");
await page.locator("#remember_me").isChecked();

const v = await page.locator("//input[@value='oneway']").isChecked();
expect(v).toBe(true);
```

4. **A text control's value**

   A value is an HTML attribute of an input-field. So in Playwright, use the
   `getAttribute` method on the `value` attribute.

   ```
   const userName = await page.locator("#username").getAttribute("value");
   expect(userName).toEqual("agileway");
   ```

Test Scripts

Selenium RSpec

```
it "User can enter passenger details" do
  driver.find_element(:id, "username").send_keys("agileway")
  driver.find_element(:name, "password").send_keys("testwise")
  driver.find_element(:name, "commit").click
  expect(page_text).to include("Signed in!")
  driver.find_element(:xpath, "//input[@value='oneway']").click
  Selenium::WebDriver::Support::Select.new(
   driver.find_element(:name, "fromPort")).select_by(:text, "Sydney")
  Selenium::WebDriver::Support::Select.new(
   driver.find_element(:name, "toPort")).select_by(:text, "New York")
  driver.find_element(:xpath, "//input[@value='Continue']").click
  expect(page_text).to include("Sydney to New York")
  driver.find_element(:name, "passengerFirstName").send_keys("Bob")
  driver.find_element(:name, "passengerLastName").send_keys("Tester")
```

```
  driver.find_element(:xpath, "//input[@value='Next']").click
  expect(driver.find_element(:name, "holder_name")["value"]).to eq("Bob Tester")
end
```

Playwright Test

```
test('User can select one way trip', async () => {
  await page.fill("#username", "agileway");
  await page.fill("#password", "testwise");
  await page.click("input:has-text('Sign in')");
  const flashText = await page.textContent("#flash_notice")
  expect(flashText).toEqual('Signed in!');

  await page.locator("//input[@value='oneway']").click();
  await page.locator("select[name='fromPort']").selectOption({label: 'Sydney'});
  await page.selectOption("select[name='toPort']", { label: 'New York' });
  await page.click("//input[@value='Continue']");
  const pageText = await page.textContent("body");
  expect(pageText).toContain("Sydney to New York");

  await page.fill("input[name='passengerFirstName']", "Bob");
  await page.fill("input[name='passengerLastName']", "Tester");
  await page.click("//input[@value='Next']");
  expect(await page.locator("input[name='holder_name']").getAttribute("value"))\
.toEqual("Bob Tester");
});
```

11: Various ways of execution test scripts

By now, you should have three test script files (5 test cases) in a test project. After completing a small scripting task, we will show you various ways to execute a single test case, one test script, and multiple test scripts in a folder.

Exercise 11

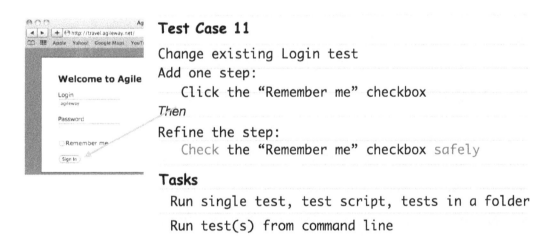

Test Case 11

Change existing Login test
Add one step:
    Click the "Remember me" checkbox
Then
Refine the step:
    Check the "Remember me" checkbox safely

Tasks
    Run single test, test script, tests in a folder
    Run test(s) from command line

A checkbox has two states: **checked** and **unchecked**. If a checkbox is already checked, selecting it again will uncheck it.

Learning Objectives

- Review

    - Run individual test case

- Run test script
- Check a control's state

• Add Conditional in scripts: `if` and `unless`
• Run all test scripts in a folder
• Run test scripts from the command line

Tasks

Task 1. Check/Uncheck a checkbox

The following statement clicks a checkbox regardless of its state, it is more like a toggling operation.

```
driver.find_element(:id, "remember_me").click
```

Please note that we cannot blindly retry (*we will cover this topic later*) this kind of test step, as it might result in an undesired control's state.

Task 2. Check/Uncheck a checkbox safely (Selenium)

To safely check a checkbox, we need to check its current state first, using `element.selected?` in Selenium. Only if it is not checked, click the checkbox.

```
elem = driver.find_element(:id, "remember_me")
if not elem.selected?
  elem.click
end
```

or

```
elem = driver.find_element(:id, "remember_me")
elem.click unless elem.selected?
```

Task 3. Check/Uncheck a checkbox safely (Playwright)

In Playwright, we can use `isChecked()` to determine if a checkbox is checked. The simplest way to check a checkbox is with the `click()` function.

```
if (!await page.isChecked("#remember_me")) {
  await page.locator("#remember_me").click();
}
expect(await page.locator("#remember_me").isChecked()).toBe(true);
```

Playwright has built in safe checkbox operations - `check()` will click on an unchecked checkbox but won't change an already checked checkbox. Similarly `uncheck()` will only click the checkbox if it is already checked.

```
await page.locator("#remember_me").check();
await page.check("#remember_me"); // will not do anything
expect(await page.locator("#remember_me").isChecked()).toBe(true);``

await page.locator("#remember_me").uncheck();
await page.uncheck("#remember_me"); // will not do anything
expect(await page.isChecked("#remember_me")).toBe(false);
```

We recommend using Playwright's built-in `check()` and `uncheck()` as they handle the safe check/uncheck for you.

Knowledge Point: Various Ways to Execute Tests

A Test Automation Engineer needs to understand the different test execution modes for various purposes.

- **One individual test case**

  The most frequently used test execution mode is for developing, debugging, stabilizing, refining, or refactoring a single test case.

- **A test script file (all test cases in it)**

  Once satisfied with individual test cases, execute the test script file (if it contains multiple test cases) to verify there are no dependencies or side effects that could impact the reliability of test executions.

- **Selected test scripts in a specific folder**

  Typically, rerun a small number of recently failed tests after fixing the issues.

- **All test scripts in a specific folder**

  To perform quality checks on the app, such as regression testing.

Execute Tests in a Testing Tool

In this context, a testing tool refers to software that test automation engineers use to develop, run, and debug automated end-to-end test scripts. The primary goal of executing tests in the testing tool is to create high-quality test scripts, not to find defects in the application (although it can identify them, it is not the main purpose). To find defects, it's more effective to run tests on a Continuous Testing server.

TestWise

TestWise executes tests in the same way across various frameworks, including RSpec, Pytest, and Playwright. Below, we use Selenium WebDriver RSpec as an example.

Run an individual test case

Both of the following methods function identically.

- Right-click within one test case, then select the first option in the context menu.

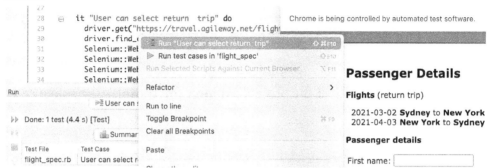

- Move the caret to a line within a test case, click the "run single test case" icon (indicated below) on the toolbar.

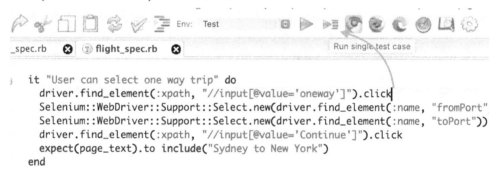

Run test script file

The following three methods all function the same.

- Click the blue play button (indicated below) on the toolbar.

- Right-click within one test case, then select the second option in the context menu.

```
it "User can select one way trip" do
  driver.find_element(:xpath, "//input[@value='oneway']").click
  Selenium::WebDriver::Support::Select.new(driver.find_element(:name, "fromPort"))
  Selenium::WebDriver::Support::Select.new(driver.find_element(:name, "toPort")).s
  driver.find_element(:xpath,
  expect(page_text).to includ
end
```

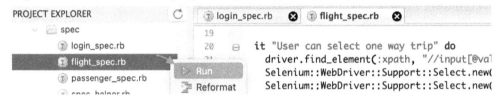

- **Right-click the file in the project explorer (on the left) and select "Run file".**

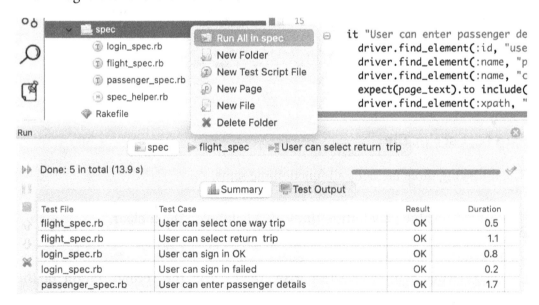

Run all test scripts in a folder

You might have noticed, by default, all our RSpec test scripts are under the "spec" folder. Right-click the folder and select "**Run All in ...**" .

Test File	Test Case	Result	Duration
flight_spec.rb	User can select one way trip	OK	0.5
flight_spec.rb	User can select return trip	OK	1.1
login_spec.rb	User can sign in OK	OK	0.8
login_spec.rb	User can sign in failed	OK	0.2
passenger_spec.rb	User can enter passenger details	OK	1.7

Please note: TestWise will only run *_spec.rb files in the mode, excluding the special debugging_spec.rb.

We don't recommend doing this frequently, as it takes time and prevents you from using the computer. It's much more efficient to run the test suite on a Continuous Testing server, such as BuildWise. For more information, check out the book: Practical Continuous Testing[1].

Visual Studio Code

VS Code is a general-purpose programming editor. With the right extensions installed, you can execute RSpec and Playwright tests directly within it.

Check for the Appendix 1 for executing Playwright tests in VS Code.

Execute Tests in a Command Window or Terminal

Up to this point, we've been executing test scripts in TestWise or Visual Studio Code, which introduces a dependency. Dependencies can be limiting, and the fewer we have, the better. The ultimate level of freedom in running test scripts is the ability to execute them directly from the command line.

> Here we set aside considerations of productivity and focus on capability. As you may know, most commercial test automation tools require you to purchase their software to execute tests. This is no good, as we want all team members to run automated end-to-end (E2E) tests easily and frequently.

You might have seen the following black windows in movies, a hacker types some text and something happens (such as opening a door in a building). These "black windows" go by various names depending on the OS.

---

[1]https://leanpub.com/practical-continuous-testing

- **{Windows} Command Prompt, DOS Prompt**

  To start a new Command Prompt.

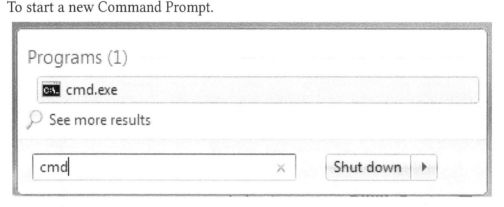

- **{Linux, macOS}: Terminal, Console**

Execute RSpec Tests

1. **Run all test cases in a script file.**

    ```
    rspec  login_spec.rb
    ```

2. **Run one specific test case (at line number).**

    ```
    rspec  login_spec.rb:20
    ```

3. **Run multiple test script files.**

    ```
    rspec  login_spec.rb another_spec.rb
    ```

4. **Run all or multiple test script files mattching a pattern.**

    Windows: `rspec spec\*_spec.rb` macOS or Linux: `rspec spec/*_spec.rb`

    Sample output:

    ```
    zhimin@Zhimins-iMac agiletravel-tests % rspec spec/*_spec.rb
    .....

    Finished in 11.94 seconds (files took 0.43474 seconds to load)
    5 examples, 0 failures
    ```

    (The 'examples' means 'test cases')

Execute Playwright Tests

Important note on Playwright test execution: You must run the tests from the root folder that contains the tests directory.

1. **Run one specific test script.**

    ```
    npx playwright test --headed tests/login.spec.ts
    ```

2. **Run one specific test case (by test name).**

```
npx playwright test --headed  -g "Admin User can sign in OK"
```

Playwright will locate the test case in the test scripts under `tests` folder.

3. **Run multiple test script files**.

```
npx playwright test --headed  04-login_ok 08-select_flight
```

The command above will execute two test scripts, `tests/04-login_ok.spec.ts` and `tests/08-select_flight.spec.ts`, simultaneously in two separate browser windows.

12: Payment Test (AJAX)

Continuing with AgileTravel, after selecting the flight and entering the passenger details, proceed with the payment using a credit card.

Exercise 12

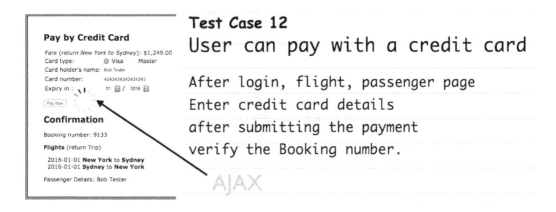

Pay by Credit Card

Fare *(return New York to Sydney)*: $1,249.00
Card type: ⊙ Visa   Master
Card holder's name: Bob Tester
Card number: 4242424242424242
Expiry in :   \\\ /   01 📅 / 2018 📅
[Pay now]

Confirmation

Booking number: 9133

Flights (return Trip)

  2016-01-01 **New York** to **Sydney**
  2016-01-01 **Sydney** to **New York**

Passenger Details: Bob Tester

AJAX

Test Case 12
User can pay with a credit card

After login, flight, passenger page
Enter credit card details
after submitting the payment
verify the Booking number.

Learning Objectives

- Review

  - Create a new test script via cloning
  - XPath locators

- AJAX Testing

  - Fixed Waits
  - Selenium Explicit Waits
  - Zhimin's way of handling waits in Ruby

- Print out data from the test script

Test Design

- Log in and select a one-way flight
- Enter passenger details
- Provide credit card information
- Click the "Pay Now" button
- Verify that a booking number is returned

Tasks

You should be comfortable with all the test steps except the last one. Why? Because it involves an AJAX request.

Task 1: Create a new test script that completes all the steps outlined in the test design.

```
16    it "User can pay with credit card" do
17        driver.find_element(:id, "username").send_keys("agileway")
18        driver.find_element(:name, "password").send_keys("testwise")
19        driver.find_element(:name, "commit").click
20        expect(page_text).to include("Signed in!")
21        driver.find_element(:xpath, "//input[@value='oneway']").click
22        Selenium::WebDriver::Support::Select.new(driver.find_element(:name, "fromPort")).select_by(:text, "Sydney")
23        Selenium::WebDriver::Support::Select.new(driver.find_element(:name, "toPort")).select_by(:text, "New York")
24        driver.find_element(:xpath, "//input[@value='Continue']").click
25        expect(page_text).to include("Sydney to New York")
26        driver.find_element(:name, "passengerFirstName").send_keys("Bob")
27        driver.find_element(:name, "passengerLastName").send_keys("Tester")
28        driver.find_element(:xpath, "//input[@value='Next']").click
29
30        driver.find_element(:xpath, "//input[@value='visa']").click
31        driver.find_element(:name, "card_number").send_keys("4242424242424242")
32        driver.find_element(:xpath, "//input[@value='Pay now']").click
33        expect(page_text).to include("Booking number")
34    end
```

Test File	Test Case	Result	Duration
12-payment_spec.rb	User can pay with credit card	Failed	1.7

Done: 1 test (7.1 s), Failed: 1 [Test]

Figure 12. The last assertion step failed.

The last step, if running again in TestWise debugging mode, passed.

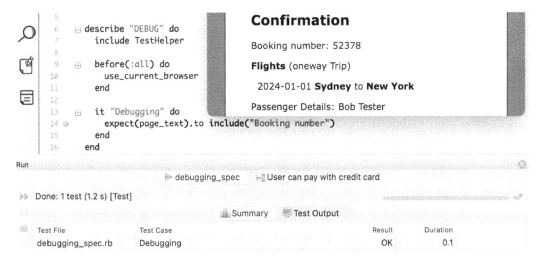

Also, we could see the booking number in the browser window.

To understand why, we suggest you running the test case (not in TestWise debugging mode) a few times and pay attention to the last page. (*Your test execution maybe pass sometimes*)

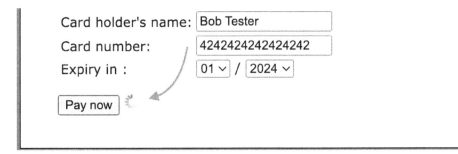

Figure 13. Ajax loading animation

The screenshot above shows the AgileTravel payment page at the moment the assertion was performed for one test execution. As you can see, the booking number had not yet been displayed, which is why the assertion step failed. However, when we ran the assertion step in TestWise's debugging mode, the booking number section was already visible, which is why it passed.

Yes, the issue was caused by a delay. We introduced random delays in the AgileTravel test suite to simulate real-world scenarios, which explains why the test occasionally passes.

Knowledge Point: "Flaky Tests"

If you've worked in end-to-end (E2E) test automation, you're likely familiar with the term "Flaky Tests". According to the Google Testing Blog, a flaky test is an automated test that "exhibits both a passing and a failing result with the same code" (Google Testing Blog). Our payment test case (the last assertion step) exhibiits this behavior.

16% of tests are flaky at Google

"Almost 16% of our tests have some level of flakiness associated with them! This is a staggering number; it means that more than 1 in 7 of the tests written by our world-class engineers occasionally fail in a way not caused by changes to the code or tests." — (Google Testing Blog[1], 2016)

The term "Flaky Tests" is relatively new in E2E test automation and wasn't as widely recognized until the rise of dynamic modern websites, as seen in our payment test case. In contrast, we had no such issues in our "User Login," "Select Flight," and "Enter Passenger" test scripts.

Unfortunately, many test automation efforts have failed, with "Flaky Tests" often used as a convenient, albeit weak, excuse. All too often, incompetence is masked by blaming the automation framework. You've likely heard false claims like "Selenium tests are flaky." Some companies have even exploited this narrative to promote their commercial products under false pretenses.

On 2024–05–04, David Burns, Chair of the Browser Testing and Tools Working Group (W3C), published an article titled "Flakiness isn't from your test framework[2]"

---

[1] https://testing.googleblog.com/2016/05/flaky-tests-at-google-and-how-we.html
[2] https://www.linkedin.com/pulse/flakiness-isnt-from-your-test-framework-david-burns-bfplc/

to criticize an article by Gleb Bahmutov, ex-principal engineer for Cypress, who claimed *"the way cypress works and not using transport layers like playwright or WebDriver based frameworks makes its tests less flaky"*. David wrote: *"That's 100% not the reason your tests are flaky. I'm not going to lie, this shocked me that Gleb would say this"*. He continued *"The reason your tests are flaky is more down to how you interpret the UI and how the browser runs the code, or to put in a different way, you're thinking about your synchronous steps of a test while they're running in an asynchronous way. This mismatch leads to flakiness."*

Selenium tests, if well written, of course not flaky. Otherwise, how could companies like Facebook—and even my own—successfully achieve "daily production releases" through automated testing with Selenium?

> "Facebook is released twice a day, and keeping up this pace is at the heart of our culture. With this release pace, automated testing with Selenium is crucial to making sure everything works before being released." — DAMIEN SERENI, Engineering Director at Facebook, at Selenium 2013 conference[3].

Here are the facts:

- There is a general lack of E2E test automation knowledge, as it is rarely taught at universities, and software companies rarely reach out for help for training and coaching.
- The so-called "Selenium Killer," Cypress, has been overtaken by Playwright in the JavaScript testing community.
- Selenium WebDriver continues to be the dominant web automation framework.

Before diving into the solution, it's important to first understand AJAX requests.

Knowledge Point: AJAX

AJAX (Asynchronous JavaScript and XML") makes websites dynamic. You must have seen it before (the loading animated image), such as sending an email in Gmail.

---

[3] https://2014.seleniumconf.in/2013/speakers/index.html

AJAX makes test automation more challenging. To understand that, please compare two types of HTTP requests.

1. **Normal HTTP Request**

In this mode, the test script interacts with the web app synchronously. In other words, test step 2 will be only executed after test step 1's response is fully returned. That's how we have been writing the test scripts so far. By the way, this is the default and natural style.

2. **AJAX Request**

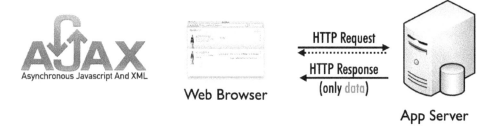

In AJAX mode, a dummy response (my term, strictly not correct terminology) is returned immediately. The actual data will be sent later. From test automation's point of view, if test step 1 invokes an AJAX request (such as clicking the 'Pay now' button on AgileTravel's payment page), test step 2 starts immediately (after receiving the dummy response). However, Test Step 1's actual response is not received yet. Most likely, the upcoming test steps will fail.

The Solution: Wait for the full response.

Please note, besides AJAX, dynamic operations on websites (by running JavaScript) can cause so-called 'flakness' in automated test execution.

Knowledge Point: Waiting in Selenium

(1) Fixed wait

```
sleep 10
expect(page_text).to include("Booking number")
```

(2) Selenium's Explicit Waits

```
wait = Selenium::WebDriver::Wait.new(:timeout => 10) # seconds
wait.until { page_text.include?("Booking number") }
```

(3) Using Ruby's built-in feature

```
try_for(10) { expect(page_text).to include("Booking number") }
```

We wait after triggering an AJAX request, such as when executing `driver.find_element(:id, "pay_button").click`.

1. **Fixed waits**

    Pause the test execution for a fixed amount time, in seconds. Then proceed to the next step.

    ```
    sleep(10)
    expect(page_text).to include("Booking number")
    ```

    The drawback of using a "fixed wait" is clear: it slows down test execution. Even if the AJAX response is returned faster, say in 3 seconds for the above operation, the test execution will still unnecessarily wait for the full 10 seconds.

2. **Explicit waits**

    ```
    wait = Selenium::WebDriver::Wait.new(:timeout => 10)
    wait.until { page_text.include?("Booking number")  }
    ```

    Some readers might wonder, "Does Implicit Wait exist?" Yes, it does. However, we believe testers should avoid using it. Similar to the "auto-waits" promoted by newer frameworks and tools, it can often lead to more problems than it solves. In fact, Zhimin has never used Implicit Waits in real testing projects.

3. **Zhimin's 'try_for', using Ruby's built-in feature to do polling**

   Technically, Explicit Waits are effective, but many Selenium testers either neglect to use them or use them incorrectly. Zhimin invented this approach in 2011 and has been using it ever since.

   ```
   try_for(10) { driver.find_element(:id, "booking_number")}
   ```

   Essentially, retry every second for up to 10 seconds.

   A tester can quickly add this wait time by using the TestWise snippet. Simply type `tf`, press the Tab key, and enter the desired wait time (in seconds). Watch the video below to see how simple it is!

   Video demo: Added Retry in TestWise[4]

4. **Fluent waits** (introduced in Selenium v4, ~2023)

   This newly added waiting strategy is similar to Zhimin's approach.

   ```
   wait = Selenium::WebDriver::Wait.new(timeout: 10, interval: 1)
   wait.until { ... }
   ```

Why Zhimin Invented the `try_for` Approach

Selenium Explicit waits, while works well, has some non-technical drawbacks:

- It breaks the flow, a bit. *Now with two line statements.*
- A change of statement. `expect(page_text).to include("Booking number")` to `page_text.include?("Booking number")`.
- Slow, requires more typing.

The advantages of Zhimin's try_for approach:

---

[4]https://youtu.be/oVglo9eu3L8

- Fast, if using TestWise snippet, as shown in the video.
- Concise and more readable.
- Logical. *Focus the test step first, then add the waiting handling, quickly.*
- Versatile. *Add retry any (& multiple) test steps.*

Nearly all Zhimin's mentees love using this. However, there are two minor constraints:

1. Test scripts must be in Ruby (*not limited to Selenium, we used this for Appium tests too*).
2. TestWise IDE makes adding this super-quick and fun.

Task 2: Make the test case reliable

Choose one of the above waiting strategies to ensure the reliability of the final assertion step.

Run the test case multiple times to ensure it passes consistently in every run.

Task 3: Assert booking number

The above assertion "Checking the 'Booking Number' label" is not ideal. Refine it as follows:

- Retrieive the booking number.
- Verify its length.
- Print out the booking nubmer.

```
puts(driver.find_element(:id, "booking_number").text)
```

Note: Since the booking number varies each time, we cannot assert its exact value. Verifying its length is sufficient.

Task 4: Implement all four Waits

Implement all four waiting approaches in this test script, in four separate test cases.

Hint: using `before(:each)` block well.

Playwright

1. **Fixed waits**

   ```
   await page.waitForTimeout(10000);
   ```

   Wait for the given number of milliseconds. 1000 milliseconds = 1 second.

2. **"Auto-Waits"**

   One key selling points of Cypress and Playwright, often highlighted, is its so-called "Auto-Waits." According to some so-called marketing videos, users supposedly don't need to worry about handling waits for dynamic or AJAX operations. However, this is far from the truth.

   Let's see a working Playwright version for assertion step of this exercise.

   ```
   driver.find_element(:xpath, "//input[@value='Pay now']").click
   const bookingNumber = await page.locator("#booking_number").textContent();
   expect(bookingNumber.length).toEqual(5);
   ```

   It worked, without waits! However, the so-called 'auto-waits' is not really auto. If you blindly trust it, you'll inevitably invite problems in real test automation, beyond just simple demos.

   There is a `timeout` entry in `playwright.config.ts`, default to 30 seconds.

   ```
   timeout: 30000,
   ```

   Seasoned testers will immediately raise concerns upon seeing this. Let's conduct a quick experiment: we set the timeout to two seconds (`timeout: 2000`) and run the same test script (unchanged) five times. Out of those five runs, three failed (the delay was randomly set between 1 to 9 seconds).

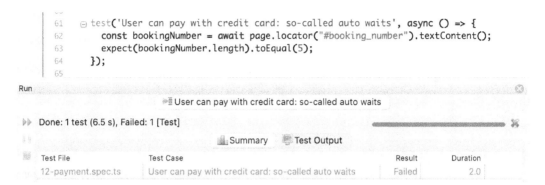

Figure 14. Test execution failed, test case execution stopped after 2 seconds

Now the test execution is **flaky**. This situation is much worse then without so-called 'auto-waits'.

It turns out that the so-called "auto-waits" are not designed to handle ideal scenarios—theey are great for demonstrations but impractical in real-world testing. In fact, Zhimin implemented a similar utility in his own RWebSpec wrapper framework over a decade ago but later realized it was a mistake and ultimately discarded it.

In addition to issue with the timeout setting, there are other problems with the so-called "Auto-Wait." For instance, even with a high timeout value configured, the below assertion step failed immediately.

```
pageText = await page.textContent("body");
expect(pageText).toContain("Booking number");
```

Why? Because, to Playwright, the body element already exists. It isn't a previously non-existent element, so Playwright does not trigger the "auto-wait" mechanism. Yuck!

With Zhimin's "try_for" approach, testers can effortlessly incorporate wait handling without thinking.

Some advocates of Cypress or Playwright might argue, "But you can't say this auto-wait is wrong; it does help testers, especially beginners." However, Zhimin speaks from experience in successful E2E test automation: developing and, more importantly, maintaining a large E2E test suite that runs daily as part of regression testing. In that context, this kind of "auto-wait" introduces more problems and frustrations.

3. **Print out text in Javascript**

```
const bookingNumber = await page.locator("#booking_number").textContent();
console.log("booking number: " + bookingNumber)
```

Test Scripts

Selenium RSpec

```
describe "Payment" do
  before(:all) do
    @driver = Selenium::WebDriver.for(browser_type, browser_options)
    driver.get("https://travel.agileway.net")
    driver.find_element(:id, "username").send_keys("agileway")
    driver.find_element(:name, "password").send_keys("testwise")
    driver.find_element(:name, "commit").click
  end

  after(:all) do
    driver.quit unless debugging?
  end

  before(:each) do
    driver.get("https://travel.agileway.net")
    driver.find_element(:xpath, "//input[@value='oneway']").click
    Selenium::WebDriver::Support::Select.new(driver.find_element(:name, "fromPo\
rt")).select_by(:text, "Sydney")
    Selenium::WebDriver::Support::Select.new(driver.find_element(:name, "toPort\
")).select_by(:text, "New York")
    driver.find_element(:xpath, "//input[@value='Continue']").click
    driver.find_element(:name, "passengerFirstName").send_keys("Bob")
    driver.find_element(:name, "passengerLastName").send_keys("Tester")
    driver.find_element(:xpath, "//input[@value='Next']").click
    driver.find_element(:xpath, "//input[@value='visa']").click
    driver.find_element(:name, "card_number").send_keys("4242424242424242")
    driver.find_element(:xpath, "//input[@value='Pay now']").click
```

```
  end

  it "User can pay with credit card: fixed waits" do
    sleep 10
    expect(page_text).to include("Booking number")
  end

  it "User can pay with credit card: Explicit waits" do
    wait = Selenium::WebDriver::Wait.new(:timeout => 10)
    wait.until { page_text.include?("Booking number") }
  end

  it "User can pay with credit card: Zhimin's try_for approach" do
    try_for(10) { expect(page_text).to include("Booking number") }
  end

  it "User can pay with credit card: Fluent waits" do
    wait = Selenium::WebDriver::Wait.new(timeout: 10, interval: 1)
    wait.until { page_text.include?("Booking number") }
    booking_number = driver.find_element(:id, "booking_number").text
    puts("booking number: " + booking_number)
  end
end
```

⯈ 12-payment_spec

▷▷ Done: 4 in total (26.6 s) [Test]   ✓

⊩ Summary   🖹 Test Output

Test File	Test Case	Result	Duration
12-payment_spec.rb	User can pay with credit card: fixed waits	OK	11.0
12-payment_spec.rb	User can pay with credit card: Explicit waits	OK	4.9
12-payment_spec.rb	User can pay with credit card: Zhimin approach	OK	1.3
12-payment_spec.rb	User can pay with credit card: Fluent waits	OK	3.9

Figure 15. Test results: The first method, fixed waits, is the slowest as it unnecessarily pauses test execution

Playwright Test

```javascript
test.beforeAll(async ({ browser }) => {
  page = await browser.newPage();
  await page.goto(Helper.site_url());

  await page.fill("#username", "agileway");
  await page.fill("#password", "testwise");
  await page.click("input:has-text('Sign in')");
  const flashText = await page.textContent("#flash_notice")
  expect(flashText).toEqual('Signed in!');
});

test.afterAll(async () => {
  await page.close();
});

test.beforeEach(async () => {
  await page.goto(Helper.site_url());
  await page.locator("//input[@value='oneway']").click();
  await page.locator("select[name='fromPort']").selectOption({label:'Sydney'});
  await page.selectOption("select[name='toPort']", { label: 'New York' });
  await page.click("//input[@value='Continue']");
  let pageText = await page.textContent("body");
  expect(pageText).toContain("Sydney to New York");

  await page.fill("input[name='passengerFirstName']", "Bob");
  await page.fill("input[name='passengerLastName']", "Tester");
  await page.click("//input[@value='Next']");

  await page.click("//input[@value='visa']");
  await page.fill("input[name='card_number']", "424242424242424242");
  await page.click("//input[@value='Pay now']");
});

test.afterEach(async () => {
});

test('User can pay with credit card: fixed waits', async () => {
  await page.waitForTimeout(10000);
  const pageText = await page.textContent("body");
  expect(pageText).toContain("Booking number");
```

```
});

test('User can pay with credit card: fluent waits', async () => {
  const bookingNumber = await page.locator("#booking_number").textContent();
  expect(bookingNumber.length).toEqual(5);
  console.log("booking number: " + bookingNumber)
});

test('User can pay with credit card: contains check failed', async () => {
  // This doesn't work - fails immediately
  pageText = await page.textContent("body");
  expect(pageText).toContain("Booking number");
});
```

13: Sony Playstation Login Test

We will write a user login test for the Sony PlayStation Store. Unlike the simpler login page of AgileTravel, this example reflects a real, modern website, similar to many others. Please note that the PlayStation Store is a public site beyond our control, so the site may change when you are testing it.

Exercise 13

Test Case #13

User Login Test (failed)

Test Data
  Site URL: https://store.playstation.com

Click Sign in link on the top
Enter a random user id
Click "Next"
Enter a random password
Click "Sign in" button
No need assertion

Learning Objectives

- Review

  - New Test Project
  - Add waiting to test steps

- Using text() in XPath.
- Using the parent node in XPath to be more specific.

- Using an element's `placeholder` attribute in XPath.
- Playwright's timeout on individual steps: {timeout: ms}

Tasks

Task 1. Click the "Sign In"

Right-click the "Sign In" button and inspect.

This is not a hyperlink (`<a href`), we cannot use the LINK_TEXT locator. Within the identified SPAN tag, there are no easy identifiers such as ID, NAME, or even a good attribute for identification.

```
<button data-qa="web-toolbar#signin-button">
  <span class="psw-fill-x psw-t-truncate-1 psw-l-space-x-2 ">Sign In</span>
</button>
```

The element's classes `psw-fill-x` are all quite generic, i.e., which are used by many other elements, so we can't use them.

Therefore, this leads to the natural thought to use the text `Sign In`. We can use it in XPath as below.

```
driver.find_element(:xpath, "//span[text()='Sign In']").click
```

The meaning of the above XPath expression: find any element that matches this condition: its tag name is span and its text equals `Sign In`.

It works.

Task 2. Stabilize the Ppath expression

 When working on web test automation step, get it working first, then stablize and optimize it later.

The below XPath locator works on this page.

```
driver.find_element(:xpath, "//span[text()='Sign In']")
```

But not optimal. If a programmer adds the following HTML fragment (an introduction text).

```
<p>No account, please click <span class='highlight'>Sign In</span></p>
```

Then our test statement would locate this one, not the button on the top bar.

Solution: prefix the parent node to make it more specific.

```
driver.find_element(:xpath, "//button/span[text()='Sign In']")
```

Task 3. Locate the "Sign-In ID (Email Address)" text box

On the sign in page, right-click the "Sign-In ID (Email Address)" text box and inspect.

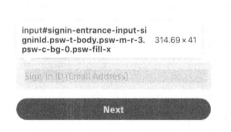

```
<input data-qa="#input"
class="psw-t-body psw-m-r-3
psw-c-bg-0 psw-fill-x" id=":
ignin-entrance-input-signin]
d" type="email" placeholder=
"Sign-In ID (Email Address)'
maxlength="64" autocomplete=
"username webauthn"
value> == $0
```

```
<input data-qa="#input" class="psw-t-body psw-m-r-3 psw-c-bg-0 psw-fill-x"
 id="signin-entrance-input-signinId" type="email"
 placeholder="Sign-In ID (Email Address)"
 maxlength="64" autocomplete="username webauthn" value="">
```

Which locator to choose? A logical choice is to use the ID locator, "signin-entrance-input-signinId". Yes, it is a good choice. Here, we recommend another maybe slightly better one, using the placeholder attribute as it matches the text shown on the screen.

```
elem = driver.find_element(:xpath,
          "//input[@placeholder='Sign-In ID (Email Address)']")
elem.send_keys("james@testwisely.com")
```

Task 4. Add Waiting (Selenium)

Work out the steps in TestWise debugging mode. Then copy the steps over to the test script. Run it.

```
17    it "Login" do
18        driver.find_element(:xpath, "//button/span[text()='Sign In']").click
19        driver.find_element(:xpath, "//input[@placeholder='Sign-In ID (Email Address)']").send_keys("james@testwisely.com")
20        driver.find_element(:id, "signin-entrance-button").click
21        driver.find_element(:id, "signin-password-input-password").send_keys("test01")
22        driver.find_element(:id, "signin-password-button").click
23    end
```

Login

Done: 1 test (14.1 s), Failed: 1 [Test]

Summary   Test Output

```
1) PlayStation Login
    Failure/Error: driver.find_element(:id, "signin-password-input-password").send_keys("test01")
    Selenium::WebDriver::Error::NoSuchElementError:
      no such element: Unable to locate element: {"method":"css selector","selector":"#signin\-password\-input\-password"}
```

The test failed on Line 21: trying to enter the password. The error message: Selenium::WebDriver::Error::NoSuchElementError.

But this step worked in the TestWise debugging mode. The most likely reason: AJAX or dynamic (with JavaScript) page. The solution is simple: add dynamic wait (see Ex12).

Move the caret to the beginning of Line 21 type tf, a Tab key, then enter 3 (the wait time). Get the following:

```
try_for(3) { driver.find_element(:id, "signin-password-input-password").send_ke\
ys("test01") }
```

This would fix it.

After submitting the login, I found that the PlayStation site failed our test (against normal expectations). Maybe PlayStation shall hire a good automated tester like you!

Figure 16. An abnormal error message when trying to login with an invalid user, as of 2024-12-14.

It seemed that we found a defect on the Sony PlayStation site. Maybe Sony should invest in E2E test automation.

Task 4. Add Waiting (Playwright)

In Playwright, each step can have it's own specified timeout with the optional `timeout` argument. The value for the timeout is in milliseconds.

e.g.

```
await page.locator("#signin-password-input-password").fill("t01",
    {timeout: 30000});
```

The timeout determines how long it takes for Playwright to recognise an element is not there before failing.

Test Script

Selenium WebDriver + RSpec

```
it "Playstation Store Login" do
  driver.find_element(:xpath, "//button/span[text()='Sign In']").click
  try_for(3) {
    driver.find_element(:xpath,
        "//input[@placeholder='Sign-In ID (Email Address)']")
      .send_keys("james@testwisely.com")
  }
  driver.find_element(:id, "signin-entrance-button").click
  try_for(3) {
    driver.find_element(:id, "signin-password-input-password").send_keys("t01")
  }
  driver.find_element(:id, "signin-password-button").click
end
```

Playwright Test

```
test('Playstation Store Login', async () => {
  await page.locator("//button/span[text()='Sign In']").click({timeout: 30000})\
;
  await page.locator("#signin-entrance-input-signinId").fill("james@testwisely.\
com", {timeout: 30000});
  await page.locator("#signin-entrance-button").click();
  await page.locator("#signin-password-input-password").fill("t01",
      {timeout: 30000});
  await page.locator("#signin-password-button").click();
});
```

14: Testing Page with iFrames

Exercise 14

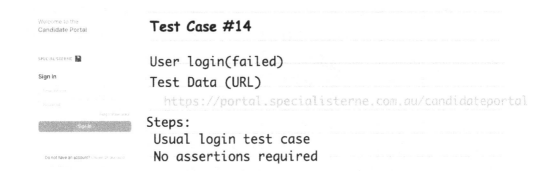

Test Case #14

User login(failed)
Test Data (URL)
https://portal.specialisterne.com.au/candidateportal

Steps:
 Usual login test case
 No assertions required

Learning Objectives

- Add a new test script file to an existing project (not by cloning)

  - start with a web page on a different site

- Identify frame
- Drive controls in a frame
- Back to main content exiting a frame

Tasks

Task 1. Add a new test script in a test folder

For a quick automation script, there's no need for a dedicated test project focused on a specific site. Instead, it's often more effective to maintain a utility automation project that houses various automation scripts.

In an existing project opened in TestWise, right-click the "spec" folder and select "New Test Script File".

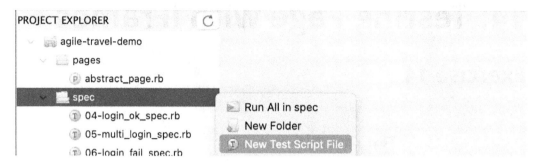

Enter a test script file name, in the example, `portal_login_spec.rb`.

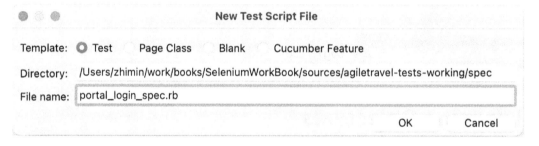

Click the "OK" button.

```
ⓘ portal_login_spec.rb      ✖
1        load File.dirname(__FILE__) + '/../test_helper.rb'
2
3  ⊟ describe "PortalLogin" do
4        include TestHelper
5
6  ⊟     before(:all) do
7          # browser_type, browser_options, site_url are defined in test_helper.rb
8          @driver = $driver = Selenium::WebDriver.for(browser_type, browser_options)
9          driver.manage().window().resize_to(1280, 720)
10         driver.get(site_url)
11       end
12
13 ⊟     after(:all) do
14         driver.quit unless debugging?
15       end
16
17 ⊟     it "Test Case Name" do
18         # driver.find_element(...)
19         # expect(page_text).to include(..)
20       end
21     end
```

A new file `portal_login_spec.rb` will be created with the above content (skeleton script filled by TestWise).

Besides the usual update to "Test Group Name" and "Test Case Name", we need to change the target web page: replace `site_url` with the specific page URL.

```
1       load File.dirname(__FILE__) + '/../test_helper.rb'
2
3     ⊟ describe "Zoho Portal" do
4           include TestHelper
5
6     ⊟     before(:all) do
7               # browser_type, browser_options, site_url are defined in test_helper.rb
8               @driver = $driver = Selenium::WebDriver.for(browser_type, browser_options)
9               driver.manage().window().resize_to(1280, 720)
10 ⇨           driver.get("https://portal.specialisterne.com.au/candidateportal")
11           end
12
13    ⊟     after(:all) do
14              driver.quit unless debugging?
15          end
16
17    ⊟     it "Portal User Sign In" do
18              # driver.find_element(...)
19              # expect(page_text).to include(
20          end
21       end
```

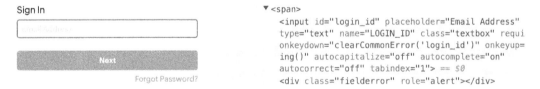

Run the test case (empty at the moment) to verify it opens the target web page OK.

Task 2. Implement the first test step: enter email address

We have done this (entering text in a text box) a few times already. Right-click and inspect it first.

The statement below should work.

```
driver.find_element(:name, "username").send_keys("bob@testwisely.com")
```

But it does not.

```
    12
 13    ⊖   it "Debugging" do
 14 ⊚          driver.find_element(:name, "username").send_keys("bob@testwisely.com")
 15        end
 16      end
    17
```

Run   ⊗

   ▶ debugging_spec   ▶ debugging_spec   ▶▤ Portal User Sign In

▶▶ Done: 1 test (1.5 s), Failed: 1 [Test]   ✖

                          ▥ Summary   ▥ Test Output

✗

F
Failures:
  1) DEBUG Debugging
     Failure/Error: driver.find_element(:name, "username").send_keys("bob@testwisely.com")
     Selenium::WebDriver::Error::NoSuchElementError:
       no such element: Unable to locate element: {"method":"css selector","selector":"*[nam
         (Session info: chrome=107.0.5304.110)
     # ./spec/debugging_spec.rb:14:in `block (2 levels) in '

Click the "Test Output" tab, and see `Selenium::WebDriver::Error::NoSuchElementError`. Why? Because that control is in a frame.

Knowledge Point: Frame and iFrame

If we scroll up the page source in the inspect panel. We can another `<HTML>` tag under `<iframe>` tag.

```
▼<div>
 ▼<iframe frameborder="0" scrolling="no" class="accountsIframe portal_iframe_s
   ignin" name="portalsigniniframe" id="portalsigniniframe" src="https://porta
   l.specialisterne.com.au/accounts/p/10014973694/signin?c…ePortalSignup.na%26s
   ervice language%3Den%26dcc%3Dtrue%26load iframe%3Dtrue" load="portal-login-f
   orm => sendPortalLoginAck" style="height: 128px;">
  ▼#document
    (https://portal.specialisterne.com.au/accounts/p/10014973694/signin?
    client p…
    ePortalSignup.na%26service language%3Den%26dcc%3Dtrue%26load iframe%3Dtrue)
     <!DOCTYPE html PUBLIC "-//W3C//DTD HTML 4.0 Frameset//EN"
     "http://www.w3.org/TR/REC-html40/frameset.dtd">
   ▼<html>
    ▶<head> … </head>
    ▼<body class="portal-login">
      <div class="bg_one"></div>
     ▶<div class="Alert"> … </div>
     ▶<div class="Errormsg"> … </div> flex
     ▼<div class="signin_container" style="visibility: visible; max-width:
       500px;">
      ▼<div class="signin_box" id="signin_flow">
       ▼<div id="signin_div">
        ▶<div class="signin_head alt_signin_head"> … </div>
        ▼<form name="login" id="login" onsubmit="javascript:return submit
          signin(this,event);" method="post" novalidate>
         ▼<div class="fieldcontainer">
          ▼<div class="searchparent" id="login_id_container">
           ▼<div class="textbox_div" id="getusername">
            ▼<span>
               <input id="login_id" placeholder="Email Address" value
               type="text" name="LOGIN_ID" class="textbox" required
               onkeydown="clearCommonError('login_id')" onkeyup="check
               ing()" autocapitalize="off" autocomplete="on"
               autocorrect="off" tabindex="1"> == $0
               <div class="fielderror" role="alert"></div>
             </span>
```

<iframe> tag specifies an inline frame. You can think of a frame is an independent web page but is included in another one.

Using frames is discouaraged. However, inline frames are still heavily used in enterprise web sites, such as Microsoft SharePoint/Dynamic 365 and WordPress. This test site is Zoho Recruit, another popular site.

From Zhimin's memory, over 50% client web apps (including in recent years) he worked on used iFrames. So, a few years ago, Zhimin was shock to know that so-called popular Cypress did not support Frames, and others. How could a 'web test automation framework/tool' be so crippled? Especially, W3C standard-based Selenium WebDriver is so much better.

Task 3. Drive controls in a frame

In the context of Test Automation, frame and inline frame are treated the same.

To drive controls within a frame in Selenium:

- switch to a frame
- drive one control in the frame
- drive another in the frame
- switch back to the main content (i.e. outside the frame)
- continue driving controls on the main page

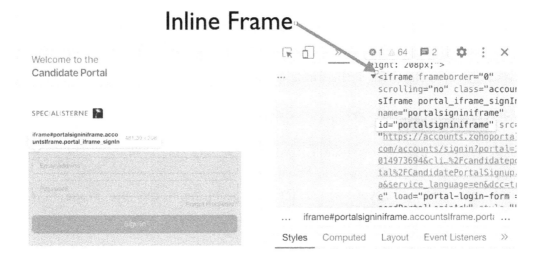

```
frame = driver.find_element(:id, "portalsigniniframe")
driver.switch_to.frame(frame)
driver.find_element(:name, "LOGIN_ID").send_keys("bob@testwisely.com")
```

A simpler way, providing the frame ID directly:

```
driver.switch_to.frame("portalsigniniframe")
```

A good habit is to switch to the main content, after completing the operations in the frame.

```
driver.switch_to.default_content
```

Handle Frames in Playwright

In Playwright, multiple frames can be "active" at once, as long as they are assigned to different variables. This means you don't need to do as much frame management as Selenium (i.e. no need to switch back to default frames explicitly).

To switch into a frame, use `page.frame`. To select which frame, you can only use the `name` attribute or the URL of the frame:

```
const frame = page.frame('portalsigniniframe');
```

```
const frame = page.frame({ url: /.*domain.*/ });
```

Then, use `frame` like you would for the `page`, i.e. can use `frame.fill()`, `frame.click()`, etc.

Test Script

Selenium WebDriver + RSpec

```ruby
before(:all) do
  @driver = Selenium::WebDriver.for(browser_type, browser_options)
  driver.get("https://portal.specialisterne.com.au/candidateportal")
end

after(:all) do
  driver.quit unless debugging?
end

it "Portal User Sign In" do
  frame = driver.find_element(:id, "portalssigniniframe")
  driver.switch_to.frame(frame)

  driver.find_element(:name, "LOGIN_ID").send_keys("bob@testwisely.com")
  driver.find_element(:id, "nextbtn").click
  try_for(3) { expect(page_text).to include("This account does not exist") }

  driver.switch_to.default_content
  # ...
end
```

Playwright Test

```javascript
test('Portal User Sign In', async () => {
  const frame = page.frame('portalsigniniframe');

  await frame.fill("#login_id", "bob@testwisely.com");
  await frame.click("#nextbtn");
  const errorMessage = await frame.textContent("//div[@class='fielderror errorl\
abel']");
  expect(errorMessage).toContain("This account does not exist");

  // Outside of frame
  await page.locator('text=Create an account').click();
  const pageText = await page.textContent(".candidate-register-form");
  expect(pageText).toContain("Register with  Specialisterne Australia");
});
```

Afterword

First of all, if you haven't downloaded the recipe test scripts from the book site[1], we strongly recommend you to do so. It is free for readers who have purchased the ebook through Leanpub.

Practice makes perfect

Like any other skills, you will get better at it by practising more. This is especially true for test automation.

Although there are only 15 exercises in this book, there are numerous variations you can explore beyond them. It's worth repeating some of these exercises—don't just sit and wait for Volumes 2 and 3 of this book series. E2E test automation requires proficiency, so make sure you master the techniques until they become second nature. Trust us, you'll definitely need that when your test suite grows large.

Zhimin has been programming/testing in Ruby for over 18 years. Zhimin can still find a better way to accomplish tasks in Ruby from time to time. And it feels good when that happens.

Apply your newly learned test automation at work

There is no more satisfying than applying newly learned test automation skills at work and get results. All software developers know that writing code is a relatively small effort, compared to debugging. E2E (UI) Test automation can be a great help in debugging, providing not only fast feedback but also preventing the introduction of regression errors.

Some senior software developers might have concerns about being seen doing software testing as they perceive software testing is lower-grade tasks.

---

[1]http://zhimin.com/books/web-test-automation-in-action-volume-1

"Testing is harder than developing. If you want to have good testing you need to put your best people in testing."

• Gerald Weinberg, software legend, in a podcast[2] (2018)

From Zhimin's experience, E2E test automation can accelerate your career by making you more productive and earn you respect from your colleagues. Of course, you can choose to keep E2E test automation to yourself, but at the very least, it will help you prevent a significant number of defects.

Automation

In addition to test automation, you can use automation scripts (without checks/assertions) to streamline your tasks. It's incredibly satisfying when a task that once took minutes can now be completed in seconds, reliably, with your own self-developed automation scripts.

You'll be surprised at how many tasks can be automated using tools like Selenium WebDriver or Playwright. Some readers may have already seen many case studies that Courtney has shared on her blog.

Learn and grow

• **Proactive learning**

After completing the exercises in Volume 1, you should be comfortable developing working Selenium/Playwright steps for medium-level scenarios. However, working ≠ good, especially in the realm of E2E test automation where maintenance efforts are substantial. Volume 2 will introduce exercises focused on Maintainable Test Design and Test Refactoring. In the meantime, you can check out more exercises on [https://agileway.substack.com/s/selenium-webdriver-training-workshop]("The Agile Way" Substack newsletter) (*without*

---

[2]https://testguild.com/tribute-gerald-weinberg/

Playwright) and the book Practical Web Test Automation with Selenium WebDriver[3].

- **Improve programming skills**

  It requires programming skills to effectively develop automated test scripts in Ruby or JavaScript. For readers with no programming background, the good news is that the programming knowledge required for writing test scripts is much less comparing to coding applications, as you have seen in this book. If you like to learn with hands-on practices, check out Learn Ruby Programming by Examples[4].

- **Running tests in Continous Testing server**

  Develop the habit to run all tests at least twice a day. To achieve that, you need to run them in a CT server. It will make test execution and detecting regression issues so much easier and quicker. Check out our book: "Practical Continuous Testing: make Agile/DevOps real[5]".

- **Teaching others**

  Teaching is another form of learning.

Best wishes for your test automation journey!

---

[3]https://leanpub.com/practical-web-test-automation
[4]https://leanpub.com/learn-ruby-programming-by-examples-en
[5]https://leanpub.com/practical-continuous-testing

Appendix 1 Test Execution Setup

By: Courtney Zhan

In Chapter 1, we covered the quick set up running a Selenium WebDriver RSpec test in TestWise and Playwright Typescript test in the command line. In this appendix, we cover with more detail.

Selenium WebDriver

Selenium WebDriver is a free and open-source web automation framework and the only one that fully conforms to the W3C WebDriver Standard. Selenium WebDriver provides official language bindings for five programming languages: Ruby, Java, C#, Python, and JavaScript. In this book, we will focus specifically on Selenium Ruby.

Install Selenium Ruby

1. Install Ruby

Installing Ruby on macOS and Linux is straightforward using their respective package managers. While the latest Ruby version is 3.3, we recommend using 3.2 for better compatibility with other libraries.

- **macOS**: can use the Ruby 2.6 that comes with the OS, better using rbenv

  rbenv[1] is a version manager tool for the Ruby programming language on Unix-like systems. It provides flexibility by allowing you to manage Ruby versions without interfering with the system-installed Ruby.

---

[1]https://github.com/rbenv/rbenv

- **Linux**: `apt-get install ruby`

- **Windows**: RubyInstaller for Windows

  Run the installer and follow the instructions. Make sure the "MSYS2 development toolchain" checkbox is checked in the installation wizard.

Verify the installation by running the command below in a terminal (or command) window.

```
ruby --version
```

2. Install the test libraries (known as gems in Ruby)

```
% gem install --no-document selenium-webdriver rspec
```

Then, you shall be ready to run a RSpec test script file (try the ones in book source):

```
% rspec your_spec.rb
```

Set up Test Execution in TestWise Standard Edition

In Chapter 1, we demonstrated how easy it is to start web test automation with TestWise Ruby Edition on Windows. For macOS and Linux users, there is the TestWise Standard Edition. In fact, after installing Ruby *(as shown above)*, we recommend using TestWise Standard Edition on all platforms, as it offers the flexibility to choose your preferred Ruby distribution.

Installing TestWise Standard Edition is straightforward and quick; you simply need to specify the execution path that includes your installed Ruby.

Below is the execution path setting for TestWise on macOS.

TestWise Settings

| General | Execution | Environment Variables | Editor | Frameworks |

Execution Path (Test frameworks, Browser drivers, Git)

/Users/zhimin/.rbenv/shims:/usr/local/bin:/usr/bin:/bin:/usr/sbin:/sbin

TestWise will invoke commands in the above PATH to run tests. Check

You can also verify the path setting by clicking the 'Check' link.

TestWise Settings

| General | Execution | Environment Variables | Editor | Frameworks |

Check the test frameworks and browser drivers installed on this machine.   Help   Detect

Test Syntax Frameworks

RSpec (Ruby)	/Users/zhimin/.rbenv/shims/rspec	3.13
Cucumber (Ruby)	/Users/zhimin/.rbenv/shims/cucumber	9.2.0
Mocha (JavaScript)	/usr/local/bin/mocha	10.2.0
pytest (Python)	/usr/local/bin/pytest	7.1.2

Browser Drivers

ChromeDriver	/usr/local/bin/chromedriver	130.0.6723.
GeckoDriver	/usr/local/bin/geckodriver	0.33.0
EdgeDriver	/usr/local/bin/msedgedriver	?

If your desired framework (or driver) is not detected, check the execution path under 'Execution' tab.

Project Preferences   OK   Cancel

Playwright

Playwright, a relatively new web automation tool developed by Microsoft. It supports multiple programming languages, including JavaScript/TypeScript, Python, Java, and .NET. In this book, we focus on the most commonly used Playwright binding: TypeScript.

Install Playwright

If you start totally fresh, run the command below.

```
npm init playwright@latest
```

The follow the prompt.

```
Need to install the following packages:
create-playwright@1.17.134
Ok to proceed? (y) y
Getting started with writing end-to-end tests with Playwright:
Initializing project in '.'
✔ Do you want to use TypeScript or JavaScript? · TypeScript
✔ Where to put your end-to-end tests? · tests
✔ Add a GitHub Actions workflow? (y/N) · false
✔ Install Playwright browsers (can be done manually via 'npx playwright install\
')? (Y/n) · true
```

This will take a few minutes, as it downloads serveral browser instances: Chrome, Firefox and Webkit.

```
Downloading browsers (npx playwright install)…
Downloading Chromium 131.0.6778.33 (playwright build v1148)
  from https://playwright...
148.6 MiB [=======              ] 36% 54.3s
```

Execute Playwright Test from Command Line

Please note that, unlike Selenium test execution, you need to run Playwright tests from the specfic folder -— the top-level folder you created when setting up the test project.

```
% cd playwright-ui-tests
```

Then, make sure the proper dependent packages are installed correctly.

```
rm -rf ./node_modules
rm package-lock.json
```

```
npm install
```

 Ruby testers might view the above steps, including setting up browser instances, as cumbersome and unnecessary. However, for JavaScript testers, these processes feel quite natural.

```
npx playwright test  tests/04-login_ok.spec.ts
```

If no errors are displayed, it means the test execution was successful. Selenium testers might be confused by the absence of test execution in a browser window. By default, Playwright runs tests in headless mode, meaning the browser is hidden. Personally, I prefer to run tests in headed mode, as it allows me to see what's happening, which is especially useful for debugging or script creation.

You can force Playwright to run in headed mode by supplying --headed.

```
npx playwright test --headed tests/04-login_ok.spec.ts
```

Set up Visual Code for Playwright Scripting

Alternatively, you can just use Visual Studio Code for Playwright using the official extension (https://playwright.dev/docs/getting-started-vscode).

Open the extensions tab in Visual Studio Code, (Command + Shift + X on Mac, Control + Shift + X on Windows) and search for "Playwright" and install the Playwright Test for VSCode extension by Microsoft.

Figure 17. Appendix Playwright Extension

After it is installed, open the Command Palette (Command + Shift + P on macOS, Control + Shift + P on Windows) and run "Test: Install Playwright". It will prompt you to download additional add-ons (playwright browsers, Github Actions support and JavaScript support). Accept these and click "OK".

Figure 18. Appendix Install Playwright

Then choose browser installation.

Figure 19. Appendix Install Playwright Options

This will open a terminal that does the installation and creates a test project.

here[2]

Figure 20. Appendix Successful Playwright Install Output

With Playwright installed and the VSCode extension, when you open a test file, you should see the green triangle "run" button next to tests.

```
TS 04-login_ok.spec.ts      ▷ 37   test('User can sign in OK', async () => {
TS 05-multi_login.spec.ts      38     await page.fill("#username", "agileway");
TS 07-login.spec.ts            39     await page.fill("#password", "testwise");
   agiletravelplaywright.tpr   40     await page.click("input:has-text('Sign in')");
   agiletravelplaywright.tws   41     const flashText = await page.locator("#flash_notice").textContent();
   buildwise.rake              42     expect(flashText).toContain('Signed in');
                               43   });
```

Figure 21. Appendix - Run Test

Click this button to execute one test case. Alternatively, move the cursor to the test and use the shortcut Command + Semi-Colon, then press C (on Windows, use Control + Semi-Colon, then C).

```
⊙ 37   test('User can sign in OK', async () => {
  38     await page.fill("#username", "agileway"); — 43ms
  39     await page.fill("#password", "testwise"); — 20ms
  40     await page.click("input:has-text('Sign in')"); — 260ms
  41     const flashText = await page.locator("#flash_notice").textContent(); — 17ms
  42     expect(flashText).toContain('Signed in'); — 1ms
  43   });
```

Figure 22. Appendix - After executing one Playwright test case in Visual Studio

The test execution shown above was successful, and you may have noticed two differences:

1. The green triangle button (Run) has been replaced with a green checkmark, indicating the test passed.
2. The test execution times are now displayed in gray text after each test step.

You may notice that Playwright runs tests in headless mode by default - meaning that you cannot see the browser as the test executes. You can alter this behaviour by changing the headless entry in the playwright.config.ts file.

```
TS playwright.config.ts          27   use: {
                                 28       /* Collect trace when retrying the
                                 29       trace: 'on-first-retry',
                                 30       // Run browser in headless mode.
                                 31       headless: false,
                                 32   },
```

Figure 23. Appendix - playwright.config.ts headless option

As of writing, Visual Studio Code does not support running tests in headed mode, instead it defaults to headless mode anyway. However, if you run tests via commandline, the configuration works. So when Visual Studio Code's Playwright extension properly supports the official config file's headless option, it will work naturally, but for now, it does not.

Appendix 2 Selenium vs. Playwright

By: Zhimin Zhan

This book covers the two leading web automation frameworks: Selenium WebDriver and Playwright. Naturally, some readers might ask, "Which one is better?"

No matter how objective we strive to be, the answer may still come across as opinionated. However, we're not avoiding the question.

The language debate often leads to nowhere.

The scripting langauge is the core factor of deciding E2E Test Automation. As we all know (and have seen), language debates between porgrammers often leaded to heated arguments and no convention at all.

Selenium WebDriver supports bindings for five languages: Ruby, Java, C#, Python, and JavaScript. Playwright supports four, with Ruby being the only language not included. Why only Ruby is omitted in Playwright offering, Zhimin's view: *"If Ruby were included, people might find Playwright unnecessary, as Selenium WebDriver with Ruby is so good!"*.

It's a waste of time for two software engineers to debate whether Language A or B is better when each only knows one of them. In this regard, Zhimin is more qualified than most software testing engineers, having authored books for each of the official Selenium binding languages.

Figure 24. Zhimin's Selenium WebDriver Recipes series

If readers don't know JavaScript or Ruby and aren't willing to learn a new language, my answer to this question won't matter to them.

Non technical factors

Zhimin, with over 15 years of experience in test automation consulting, has observed that comparisons between automation frameworks often offer little practical value, as decisions are usually made in advance. For example, if a proof of concept (POC) is led by a principal engineer who is only familiar with JavaScript, they are unlikely to consider Selenium's Ruby implementation, regardless of its objective advantages. This is simply human nature, and Zhimin has encountered this scenario numerous times.

For software professionals working in a software company, unless you hold a senior position, you proabably don't have a choice.

Framework comparsiaion

Before revealing my answer, let's clarify a key point. When it comes to E2E test automation, the primary goal is getting the job done. For example, if your team is able to develop and maintain over 200 user-story-level E2E (UI) tests and run them as regression tests daily, and your solution works well, then you can disregard others' suggestions. Ultimately, test automation is about being objective, quick judgments based on the results.

I proposed a practical, cost-effective, based-on-common-sense and quick approach for any software company looking to implement E2E test automation in this article, Test Automation and Continuous Testing Competition Week[1].

Quick and Practical Suggestions

Back to the question. My answer based your position.

1. **A startup owner**

   Selenium WebDriver + RSpec.

   Because the framework and languages for E2E testing is totally independent. Going Selenium WebDriver + RSpec certtainly increase chances to success, by a lot.

2. **Mid-level software engineer looking to introduce web test automation to the company**

   First, assess the people, current test execution efforts and the histoyr of past attempts at the company. The primary purpose for someone doing this is for promotion, right? However, if you're not careful, it could backfire. Do you have the capacity to develop and maintain 200+ automated E2E tests (regardless of language or framework)? Do you have the capacity to develop and maintain 200+ automated E2E tests (regardless of language or framework)? Our guess is that you don't. If company executives adopt your proposals but you fail to maintain even a 50-test suite, it could lead to embarrassment.

   Aside from office politics, there are other factors at play. Here, I share an interesting perspective. Many Java/JavaScript programmers dislike, even fear, Ruby. Why? Because its high productivity and the simplicity of the Ruby on Rails architecture are seen as a threat to them. This is highlighted in the book Beyond Java by Java expert Bruce A. Tate, published in 2004.

   It's often wiser to go with the flow and avoid trying to be a hero unless you're absolutely certain you're prepared. In many companies, employees commonly adopt an "another day, another dollar" mindset. In the workplace, not everything is about being right or wrong.

---

[1]https://agileway.substack.com/p/test-automation-and-continuous-testing

Take John Lasseter, the creator of Toy Story, was fired by Disney for basically promoting computer animation — a concept ahead of its time (*you can learn more in The Pixar Story documentary*). While Lasseter was undeniably correct about the future of animated films, his innovative ideas made many of his Disney colleagues (and upper management) uncomfortable.

If you are truly motivated and eager to do meaningful automated testing work but lack the capability and confidence, persuade management to engage a test automation coach for training and mentoring.

3. **Motivated learner, and have big plans, e.g. doing side hustles or building own apps, for the future**

   Selenium WebDriver + RSpec.

   Recent surveys[2] (early 2024) confirm that Selenium WebDriver continues to dominate as the leading web automation framework. More importantly, as a W3C standard supported by all major browser vendors, WebDriver ensures a reliable and future-proof investment.

   By completing the exercises in this book and trying both frameworks, you'll likely agree with us: Selenium WebDriver is much easier to learn due to its simplicity and intuitiveness. While Playwright offers some impressive features that are great for demonstrations, I can tell you that they aren't particularly useful when working with a large test suite. The quality of test scripts is what truly matters.

---

[2]https://zhiminzhan.medium.com/selenium-webdriver-is-still-the-best-web-test-automation-framework-in-2024-3c0c68d38965

Appendix 3 Practical Advice: Open to Do Both Frameworks at Work

By: Zhimin Zhan

This section is for readers who love to use Selenium WebDriver + RSpec but find themselves directed by their company to adopt Playwright Test for web test automation.

Here is my advice: **Do both**. Start with Selenium WebDriver + RSpec using TestWise IDE, then convert the test scripts to Playwright Test.

While you are processing the above suggestion, let me share a story about Courtney Zhan's internship experience.

A few years ago, right after graduating from university, Courtney began a 3-month internship at a large telecom company. The dozens of interns were assigned to different teams, a high percentage of them was given a task of testing, manual testing, of course.

Courtney completed the task quickly by developing automated E2E test scripts (*Selenium WebDriver + RSpec using TestWise, the same tech stack you have seen/used in this book*). The team lead was deeply impressed. Her tests running daily on a BuildWise CT Server (*hosted on her local machine*) provided good feedback (*detecting regression errors quickly*) to the team.

Shortly after, the team lead informed the upper management and the director overseeing the internship program. Courtney was invited to present a demonstration at a division-wide online event, which was highly praised. Following this, a senior test automation engineer in Sydney, known as the company's the "go-to" automation expert, reached out to Courtney.

After knowing the test sccripts are written in Selneium, this senior engineer said, "*While Selenium is still a proved tool for web test automation in the company, I am promoting Playwright, a better option*". Basically, he requested Courtney to use Playwright.

Courtney asked my advice. My reply was "Do both".

Long story short, Courtney did both and made two set of scripts running in BuildWise. Later, during further discussions with the senior engineer, it emerged that his Playwright test suite consisted of only about 20 simple tests that hadn't been run in months. When Courtney insisted on a demo, he attempted to run one of the tests, but it failed immediately.

Why does the "do both" approach work?

Doing E2E test automation in both frameworks by no means doubling the work, not at all.

Well-designed top-level E2E test scripts: nearly identical across languages and frameworks

Let me show you two Passenger test scripts (top level) based on Maintainable Test Design, using Page Object Model. *(This topic will be covered in Volume 2)*

Selenium WebDriver RSpec

```
load File.dirname(__FILE__) + '/../test_helper.rb'

describe "Passenger" do
  include TestHelper

  before(:all) do
    @driver = $driver = Selenium::WebDriver.for(browser_type, browser_options)
    driver.manage().window().resize_to(1280, 720)
    driver.get(site_url)
    login("agileway", "testwise") # a helper function
  end

  after(:all) do
```

```
      driver.quit unless debugging?
    end

  it "Can enter passenger details (using page objects)" do
    flight_page = FlightPage.new(driver)
    try_for(2) { flight_page.select_trip_type("oneway") }
    flight_page.select_depart_from("Sydney")
    flight_page.select_arrive_at("New York")
    flight_page.select_depart_day("02")
    flight_page.select_depart_month("May 2025")
    flight_page.click_continue

    # now on passenger page
    passenger_page = PassengerPage.new(driver)
    passenger_page.enter_first_name("Bob")
    passenger_page.enter_last_name("Tester")
    passenger_page.click_next

    expect(driver.find_element(:name, "holder_name").attribute("value")).to eq(\
"Bob Tester")
  end
end
```

Playwright Test

```
import { test, Page, expect } from '@playwright/test';
test.describe.configure({ mode: 'serial' });
var helper = require('../test_helper');

// Reuse the page among the test cases in the test script file
let page: Page;
var FlightPage = require('../pages/flight_page.js')
var PassengerPage = require('../pages/passenger_page.js')

test.beforeAll(async ({ browser }) => {
  page = await browser.newPage();
  await page.goto(helper.site_url());
  await helper.login(page, "agileway", "testwise"); // helper function
});
```

```
test.afterAll(async () => {
  await page.close();
});

test('Enter passenger details', async () => {
  let flight_page = new FlightPage(page);
  await flight_page.selectTripType("oneway")
  await flight_page.selectDepartFrom("Sydney")
  await flight_page.selectArriveAt("New York") // failed but not showing line
  await flight_page.selectDepartDay("02")
  await flight_page.selectDepartMonth("052025")
  await flight_page.clickContinue()

  let passenger_page = new PassengerPage(page);
  await passenger_page.enterFirstName("Bob")
  await passenger_page.enterLastName("Builder")
  await passenger_page.clickNext();

  const passengerName = await page.locator("[name=holder_name]").getAttribute('\
value');
  expect(passengerName).toEqual("Bob Builder")
});
```

These two are pretty similar, aren't they?

Go for Productity

Courtney is proficient in Selenium WebDriver and TestWise (*she began learning at the age of 12, because Selenium and Ruby are so easy to learn*), enabling her to develop high-quality test scripts with an efficiency never before seen in the company. The TestWise debugging mode is particularly helpful.

Once she finalized the test steps with refined locators in Selenium, converting them to Playwright TypeScript was a quick and seamless process.

This advice applies to "Playwright → Selenium WebDriver" too.

Be proactive. Focus on delivering results and being productive, rather than spending time debating frameworks, scripting languages, or complaining.

Resources

Scripts

http://zhimin.com/books/web-test-automation-in-action-volume-1

Username: `agileway`
Password: `TESTWISE24`

Log in with the above, or scan QR Code to access directly.

Books

- **Practical Web Test Automation**[1] by Zhimin Zhan

  Solving individual selenium challenges (what this book is for) is far from achieving test automation success. *Practical Web Test Automation* is the book to guide you to the test automation success.

- **Selenium WebDriver Recipes in Ruby**[2] by Zhimin Zhan

  The problem-solving guide to Selenium WebDriver with over 150 ready to run recipe test scripts.

- **API Testing Recipes in Ruby**[3] by Zhimin Zhan

  The problem-solving guide to testing API such as SOAP and REST web services.

---

[1]https://leanpub.com/practical-web-test-automation
[2]https://leanpub.com/selenium-recipes-in-ruby
[3]https://leanpub.com/api-testing-recipes-in-ruby

- **Learn Ruby Programming by Examples**[4] by Zhimin Zhan and Courtney Zhan
  Master Ruby programming to empower you to write test scripts.

- **Practical Continuous Testing**[5] by Zhimin Zhan
  The second book of Zhimin's "Practical Testing" series, focuses on how to effectively execute automated functional tests in a Continuous Testing server.

Blogs

- **The Agile Way**[6]
  The Substack Newsletter where Zhimin shares his unique insights, lessons, and best practices drawn from over 20 years of hands-on experience in end-to-end test automation, coding, and Continuous Testing.

Tools

- **TestWise IDE**[7]
  AgileWay's next-generation functional testing IDE supports Selenium Web-Driver, Appium and Playwright.

- **Visual Studio Code**[8]
  VS Code, a free and powerful source code editor from Microsoft, can be used for editing and running end-to-end (E2E) tests.

- **BuildWise Server**[9]
  AgileWay's international award-winning, free and open-source continuous testing server, purposely designed for running automated UI tests with quick feedback.

---

[4] https://leanpub.com/learn-ruby-programming-by-examples-en
[5] https://leanpub.com/practical-continuous-testing
[6] https://agileway.substack.com/
[7] http://agileway.com.au/testwise
[8] https://code.visualstudio.com
[9] http://agileway.com.au/buildwise

The photo on the book front cover:

JR East E259 Series Train on Narita Express Line in Tokyo, Japan.

Photo Taken: Zhimin Zhan
Cover Design: Courtney Zhan

www.ingramcontent.com/pod-product-compliance
Lightning Source LLC
Chambersburg PA
CBHW080527060326
40690CB00022B/5055